THE
AGENCY ROADMAP

How to build a successful and profitable agency
with predictability and certainty

JOHN PAUL

RETHINK PRESS

First published in Great Britain in 2019 by Rethink Press
(www.rethinkpress.com)

© Copyright John Paul

CONTENTS

INTRODUCTION   **1**

The nine modules of the Agency Roadmap   4

1. COMPANY DEFINING DOCUMENTS – THE BASICS   **9**

Company values   11

Customer service charter   22

Mission statement   30

2. RECRUITMENT   **43**

Recruitment questions to ask yourself   44

Always be recruiting   47

How to discover someone's values   51

The job offer   56

3. HOW TO SYSTEMISE THE BUSINESS   **63**

The operations manual   63

The art of delegation – make yourself redundant   69

Auditing   74

Review – work out what or who to fix   79

4. TRAINING YOUR STAFF   **89**

Which methods work?   92

Seven steps to developing an effective individual
training and development plan   97
Training paperwork   105

5. MANAGING STAFF   **115**
Everyone loves a routine   115
Getting – and staying – motivated   118
How to give managers a fighting chance   123

6. KEY PERFORMANCE INDICATORS   **141**
Why are KPIs important?   141
Which KPIs should you have?   144
How to present your KPIs   149

7. FINANCIAL MANAGEMENT   **153**
Profit and loss   154
Balance sheet   160
Cash flow   165
Help with your financial statements   166

8. LEADERSHIP   **169**
What to look for in a potential leader   171
Develop a training programme   177
Learn to let go   180
Five levels of leadership   183

9. PROSPECTING   **187**
What is prospecting?   188
Tips to get over rejection   191
Prospecting strategies   197

Where do you get prospects' info from?   202
Tips to becoming a top prospector   203

CONCLUSION   **209**
Do you want to learn more?   211

ACKNOWLEDGEMENTS   **213**

THE AUTHOR   **215**

INTRODUCTION

Business is tough. Add in increased legislation, staff issues, lack of sales, agents racing to the bottom with low fees, and we have an industry that is hard to operate in, let alone grow and make a decent profit in to support ourselves and our families.

Why do some businesses thrive when the vast majority in the estate agency industry struggle from month to month and seem to get nowhere? The answer, like many things, is simple: they have structure.

When we lack structure, we don't know what to do, when to do it and how to do it. No one tells us how to run our business, we just make it up as we go along. I know I did. I made so many mistakes in the beginning, I could have given up on numerous occasions, and nearly did. The difference is that I learned from those mistakes, felt the pain of them and promised never to make them again – which, of course, I duly did, but I always improved using the knowledge I'd gained.

My mistakes have allowed me to grow my business to seven branches, with over fifty staff managing 2,000 properties. We sell close to 400 houses a year, but I don't get involved in the day-to-day running of the business. In fact, I spend fewer than eight hours a month working in my agency. I'm lucky in that I get to spend my time on other business interests, including training and mentoring agents to give them structure in their business, which in turn gives them options. Options to grow and scale their agency, or just to work less, spend more time with the family, or have more fun – whatever is closest to them.

How have I been able to do this? I have designed the Agency Roadmap, a process of nine modules that, when followed and implemented, will give you the structure and clarity you need to build a successful and sustainable business rather than meandering along, seeing what happens on a day-to-day basis. This is never a good plan.

We all like structure. It's a basic human trait. We may call it routine or even habit, but knowing how to do something and doing it repeatedly will give us better results. We *can* see the wood for the trees if it's written in front of us to follow.

This book is for all estate and letting agencies, small or large, new or old, as the principles are the same, whatever stage you are in business. A phrase I like to use is 'corporate, but agile'. I've taken the best ideas that some of the larger companies across various industries operate to come up with the Agency Roadmap. I've also tested and tweaked everything contained in the book in my various businesses, some not even property related, and I only advocate what I know for a fact works. This isn't theory; this is practical advice that will make your business better, and fast.

The Agency Roadmap is a tried and tested method I designed specifically for the agency industry. It has allowed my team and I to win many awards, many industry firsts, and has elevated my business to new heights. In brief, the Agency Roadmap has made my business successful by giving my team and I the opportunities for success.

For instance, for four years in a row, at the *Sunday Times* Letting Agency of the Year awards, we have never been out of the top three for the best training and development in the whole of the UK. There's a reason for this. We have implemented our model of training and development, and the judges recognised that. Another example is that we are the only agency to have achieved Investors in People GOLD accreditation on our first attempt. This is down to the way we manage and lead the staff. In all seven locations where we have a branch, we regularly come either first or a close second in the amount of properties we let, sell or take on. We are up against the biggest of corporates in the UK with their call centres and war chests. Our success is due to the level of prospecting we maintain.

Most of us don't start off in business like Sir Alan Sugar or Richard Branson; we just get stuck in and see what happens. The Agency Roadmap stops all of that. It gives us modules to follow in our business. It breaks things down, giving us task lists to implement to take us to a better place and give our business structure.

I have written this book to make it simple to follow – it needs to be for me to understand it. Each chapter covers one of the Agency Roadmap modules and ends with a task list for you to implement in your business. You don't have to read the modules in order; you can jump straight to the chapter that is most relevant to your business currently, and then read the other chapters after that. There is no set format to follow, but I always recommend to my clients that they implement the company defining documents module first, the reason being that so many of the other modules are affected by this one. A great example of this is that we recruit based on our values and beliefs, which are essential parts of the company defining documents. We even manage – another module – based on values and beliefs.

The nine modules of the Agency Roadmap

Company defining documents

One of the most under-utilised aspects of any business, quite often seen as a wishy-washy American idea, are company defining documents. I can categorically say I don't know of one successful business that doesn't have some kind of company defining documents promoted within it.

The three main documents that are an essential part of any business are:

- **Values and beliefs** – how do you want your company to be run? What is important to you and the staff and how will you make decisions? Values and beliefs are the integral part of any business and how you want to be remembered. Run an organisation based on values and you will have a company to be proud of.
- **Mission statement** – the end game for your business. What is it that you are trying to achieve? The mission statement will keep everyone on the right path.
- **Customer service charter** – essential for giving superior customer service. This is a list of promises that, when followed both internally and externally, will deliver superior service.

Recruitment

We all know a business is only as good as its staff, so we need to ensure we recruit and retain the right people. In short, we need the right bums on the right seats. But how do we do that? How do we recruit? And when I say that 99% of businesses are getting recruiting wrong, will you be shocked?

Systems and processes

I love systems and processes – they're two of the main reasons I have grown my business to be as successful as it is. It's all down to having a set of rules that the staff follow – clearly defined rules that can't be misinterpreted.

Training and development

Once you have the best staff, you need to be able to motivate them, and giving them bespoke training and development is the best way to do so. Not increased wages; not extra holidays; not any other monetary or financial benefit. This is why companies without structure in their training and development department struggle to retain staff.

Management

The weakest part of most small and medium-sized enterprises (SMEs) is the management. Business owners are either too soft or far too hard on their staff, which results in lack of respect. Actions don't get done, things get missed, and business gets lost, all because some of the most basic management skills are missing.

Key performance indicators (KPIs)

'If you're not keeping score, you're just practising.'

ONE

COMPANY DEFINING DOCUMENTS – THE BASICS

If you build anything in life, then you need strong foundations. How many people do you know who have not had the basics in place, then have had major issues later in their business or personal life? I know literally dozens of people like this, usually the show-off types who talk about their riches and how well they are doing, but don't concentrate on getting the basics implemented. They tend to have the attitude of, 'It will never happen to me, I'm riding too high, things can't possibly go wrong'. But guess what? They can – and they always do.

In fact, I'll go so far as saying that I don't know a single person who has built a successful business without a good business foundation. The foundations are that important... but what are they?

Is it getting the right staff? No, it comes before that.

Is it getting the systems in place? No, it's before that.

Is it finding the perfect location for an office? It's even before that.

The foundations of any successful business are the company defining documents that will be the 'rules' of how it will operate for years to come. They may be there for thirty years. In fact, they may outlast the business founder.

What company defining documents do you need to have in place to set the foundations for success? There are only three, and they are:

- **Company values** – the rules by which you and your company abide, and how decisions are made.
- **Customer service charter** – the customer service promise which you and your staff make to your clients and are held accountable to.
- **Mission statement** – the overall goal stating where you want to take the company and how you will get there.

Get these three documents right and everything else will flow from them, assisting you in making business decisions.

Imagine you have a strict set of rules – let's call it a code – that you follow without exception. If a situation arises, it's simply a case of *having the staff adhere to the code*. If they do, then you succeed; if they don't, you don't. It's that simple.

You may be saying something like, 'Yes, but I'm OK. I follow my rules all the time, I just know them. There's no need to write them down or have them displayed on a poster in my office.'

I have two things to say to that:

1. There will be times when situations test your inner metal and integrity, and it won't be as easy as you may think to make a simple decision. A reminder will do you no harm.

2. Your staff. It's easy when you are the big boss in charge to make decisions, but this isn't all about you. It's about your staff. They don't always have the same way of thinking as you do, and they *will* need reminding of the rules of the game.

Company values

Why we do what we do, but more importantly, how we do it.

As business owners, we generally have, dare I say it, a higher level of emotional intelligence than others. This means we are (or should be) better at self-awareness, self-regulation, etc, and in the main we wouldn't do what we do unless we enjoyed it. Don't get me wrong, there are plenty of things that can be frustrating about running an agency, such as awkward staff, tenants, landlord and contractors. Who said this was going to be easy, eh?

We want to get up and do work which gives us satisfaction and makes us and our staff happy. A happy workforce makes for an easier life, so we want to have a connection with those we work with, regardless of whether we are the boss or not. We want to contribute and make a difference. We want a job/business that means more than what it looks like on the outside.

How do we as business owners instil that warm, fuzzy feeling in our staff? We do it by having company values and beliefs.

When researching this chapter, I must have looked at over a dozen definitions of company values and beliefs, and the *Business Dictionary* provided by far the best.

The operating philosophies or principles that guide an organisation's internal conduct as well as its relationship with its customers, partners and shareholders.

At a base level, company values and beliefs are the essence of our company's identity. They are the DNA of our company and how it operates. But the surprising thing is that many companies still don't have a set of values and beliefs. Or worse still, they have an arbitrary list of words on the wall that no one knows, recognises or follows. Basically, they are there for show.

If you are looking to create or update meaningful values and beliefs, then the first place to look is to those who are expected to live and breathe them: your staff.

Why have company values?

When you build a company around values, you will have a company to be proud of. The hardest thing is getting started.

Values must come from the top. If we, as business owners, don't believe in the company values, then how can we expect the staff to buy in to them all?

Notice I used the words 'buy in'. It doesn't mean that every staff member has to have the exact same values that you do. You may be family orientated and they may not be. You may be fiercely proud of something and they couldn't care less. They do, however, have to recognise, appreciate and follow the company values in order to work for you.

> The value of a man should be seen in what he gives and not in what he is able to receive.
>
> **Albert Einstein**

If you think about it, you wouldn't have friends whose values were misaligned to your own, so why would you work with people who don't share the same values?

What do you need your company values to do?

- **Define who you are.** If you don't have an identity or brand, you'll quickly lose direction and forget what you stand for.
- **Assist in the decision-making process.** Any significant decisions should be underpinned by your values. For example, you may need to make a hard decision about letting staff go or turning away work, but if you stay true to your values, you will make the correct decision.
- **Assist with writing the procedures.** If you write your procedures with your values in mind, you will be expecting the staff to perform in a way that is aligned with your personal and company values.

- **Provide a competitive advantage.** Values help to educate clients or customers on your unique selling point (USP), selling what makes you different.
- **Be a valuable recruitment and retention tool.** Your business doesn't have values, the people within it do. By recruiting against those values, you attract individuals who align with who you are and what you do. The Millennials defy their predecessors by ranking culture, corporate identity and benefits such as work-life balance over and above salary or location. Values will help you to attract top talent.
- **Communicate what is important.** Values influence behaviour, shaping your culture and inspiring people to action. That translates into greater productivity, innovation, and ultimately, business success.

A major advantage of having a well-designed and developed set of company values is that you can manage staff against the values. For example, in my agency, Castledene, our values are 'Be better'.

I had a professional background in a number of sports and played at national and international level, so I'm a competitive person by nature. Probably too competitive if you ask my long-suffering wife and kids, but it serves me well in other areas. I want my company and employees to be continually striving to be better at everything we do. That doesn't mean that we always have to be the best, but it does mean we have to aim to be the best and improve from our current position.

I'm also a keen nerd when it comes to how to motivate staff and get the best from them. Pretty much all of the world's leading motivational theorists say the same thing motivates people: moving towards a goal; becoming better at something. This is why at Castledene, we styled our company values around this motivational theory.

As you can see from the poster, which we have up in all our offices, it's about improving every aspect of the business:

- Give a better customer service
- Have a better attitude
- Give a better experience
- Make a better company
- Become a better you

I appreciate that these are centred around progression, achievement, etc and may not be everyone's values, but they emphasise the point that company values must be led from the top down. As business owners, we *must* drive our company values forward and have total belief in what we are presenting to our staff.

At Castledene, we will only recruit people who we feel share our values. If anyone comes in and says, 'I'm happy plodding along, not bothered about becoming better or doing my best', then we don't proceed with the interview. We score the interviewee on their values, which play a big part in the overall scoring.

How to come up with company values

Determine who should be involved. Depending on the size of your company or team, the group (or person) in charge of creating your values could be very different. It could be just you or it could be a team of people. I confess, at Castledene we cheated a little. I already had the values pretty much ironed out, but wasn't quite sure how to word them. I then got the managers involved and explained what I was doing and why I'd invited them to be part of the process.

This process highlighted that even though I didn't know exactly what the values would be, I had already attracted people with the same values as me, as every manager spoke about being the best or beating a certain competitor or always improving.

It may just be you who decides the company values if your team is small. You may drive the conversation or decision by involving others, or you may see it as more of an engagement or creative process. You have the final say, and you can decide what the values should be.

Brainstorm about what's important to you and your team. For my team, the next step was to sit down together and have a brainstorming session. Although we didn't just brainstorm ready-made values from other businesses, we did look at other companies and what their values were (some examples are coming up). We'd scheduled the meeting in advance, so that everyone could have a good think and come prepared with suggestions. We then put ideas on to a white board (bear in mind I already had a reasonable idea where I wanted this to go). The session was invaluable as it ensured that the management team bought in, having had a hand in moulding the business values.

Sit down in a quiet room and go through what you think your values are. Bear in mind that they shouldn't change; they will be with you pretty much for the rest of your working life. But you will have had them from as far back as you can remember. Your parents and how they brought you up will have a lot to do with your values.

A word of warning, though: don't pick the usual suspects of honesty, integrity, customer service excellence. Those are the standard go-to phrases that *everyone* uses. They should be a given.

What do I mean by that? If I felt the need to shout about the fact I had integrity, I would personally be a little bit embarrassed. I've always had integrity and honesty; surely that is expected of me. It's like someone asking what I did at the weekend and my reply being, 'Well, I woke up, got out of bed, brushed my teeth, had a shower...'

Get happy with your values. Become comfortable with them before speaking to your staff.

Consolidate and define. In my experience, this step took the longest – and for good reason. At this point, my team and I took twenty to twenty-five ideas that we had brainstormed, combined the similar ones and narrowed the list down to around twelve. There were some big characters in the room, so people felt strongly about certain suggestions. The funny thing was, the team was arguing (or should I say debating) over words that have the same or similar meanings. One person had brought up the word 'progression' and another 'achievement', which to me both mean that we are moving towards attaining our goals.

It was nice to see so much passion and belief around the values, even though it was a little heated at times. The process took a couple of weeks. It's not a time-bound exercise, and nor should it be. You can't put a time limit on coming up with the rules by which you and your team will forever operate.

After what seemed like an age, but in fact was only a couple of weeks, we came up with our company values. My MD and I were really happy with them and felt that they summed us both up, and how we wanted the company to operate.

Frame your values according to your team's culture. The next task is to get your values out to the staff. Again, this process will depend on your company and how you operate. Is your company a one-person band, a large single office or a multi-branch corporate?

Castledene had four branches at the time my team and I came up with our values, so we rolled them out at our monthly management meeting. It was a great and well-received process. The branch managers then filtered the values down to their staff, and as they had contributed to the values themselves, they all took extra time and care in embedding them within their branch.

Getting management buy in is certainly advisable. We made the values into large posters and we have at least two in every branch, ensuring that one is in the main office where all our customers and clients can see it, so that they know how we operate and can hold us to account. The other is in the kitchen or the training room so the staff can see it all the time, allowing it to act as a subtle reminder. I've caught people reading it time and time again. It's as though they are proud that we have values and we follow them.

I appreciate that this may feel a bit new age, but hopefully you will see how important values are as a business process. They are critical to the foundation of the business.

Live it, breathe it. Once you have a set of values and have rolled them out across your company, you need to be consistent with them. It can't be a flash-in-the-pan exercise; you can't be all for it in May, then forget about it in June. They have to be *the* rules that you follow throughout your business cycle.

Having a set of values only works if they're ideas that are going to push you and your team to excellence – so make sure you've outlined what will work for you and you are consistent. Some people won't share your values, so be prepared for some disagreements and questioning. That's fine; don't get angry or upset about it. It's natural. It's a bit like asking who the best footballer is. We all have our own opinions; just make sure you have thought of all the potential avenues that the conversation could go down. At the end of the day, you are doing your staff the courtesy of discussing your values with them. It's your business, and you don't have to listen to feedback if you don't want to – although I highly recommend you do.

Examples of company values

Here are four of my favourite company values. Use them for inspiration, but do not copy them as they won't be your own. Your values need to come from your heart, not someone else's. If you don't believe in them or share them, then you won't get excited about them, and if you don't get excited, you can't expect others to follow them.

Build-A-Bear core values are: 'Reach, learn, di-bear-sity, colla-bear-ate, give, cele-bear-ate'. I love this – this company's leaders clearly brought in their own sense of humour and identity to make the values fun. And guess what? It works. See if you can do the same.

If you have ever shopped at Ikea, you'll probably recognise that these four words scream the company's brand identity: Togetherness, cost-consciousness, respect, simplicity.

Adidas is all about winning. If you perform, have passion, show integrity and are diverse, then you will be winning. I love Adidas's values as they are similar to my own: Performance, passion, integrity, diversity.

Good old Disney is my favourite of all time: Dream, believe, dare, do. I just love the whole Disney ethos.

Walt Disney wanted anything to be possible. If you could dream it, then he said it could be achieved. If you believed it, then it could be done. Anyone who has been to Disneyland will understand that it *is* the place where dreams come true, and it's all down to Disney's values.

Disney doesn't call its customers 'customers' or 'clients'; it calls them guests, which just oozes hospitality. This value starts at the top and cascades down the company, leaving nothing and no one untouched.

If you research Disney, as I have, for customer service, then you will read countless stories which relate back to the company's values and excellent levels of service.

Customer service charter

What is this? A customer service charter is best described as a set of promises which a company follows in order to reach and deliver the best customer service possible. It's a promise that all the staff sign up to and must adhere to at all times. A bit like the values of the company, it means that when a staff member doesn't perform, you are able to measure them against it by asking a simple question: 'Do you believe that your actions aligned with the customer service charter?'

A customer service charter is important as we are in a people business, and people are *huge* on customer service. It does get bandied around a lot, customer service this and customer service that, and it will vary from person to person, so you need to have your own definition of customer service and, more importantly, what you need to do to achieve it.

At Castledene, we have two parts to our charter:

1. External. We have five promises that we always follow, which are highlighted and communicated to the customers in the form of posters in all our offices:

- Promise 1 – we will always make you feel welcome
- Promise 2 – we will understand and meet your needs
- Promise 3 – we will build relationships through professionalism and trust
- Promise 4 – we will constantly strive for improvements through innovative solutions
- Promise 5 – we take pride and enjoyment in what we do

We want to be held accountable, and on occasions have been.

It may sound like we are setting ourselves up for a fall, and when we first decided to display our promises on huge posters in each and every office, we were expecting a bit of a backlash from the staff. And some of the staff weren't happy about this and disagreed with the idea. But the good ones, the ones who already delivered superb customer service, thought it was a great idea. Why wouldn't they?

If you do what you say you will do, when you say you will do it, then you never have anything to worry about. Honestly, your staff's reaction will be the same as my staff's: some will love it and some will hate it. The ones who hate it will be the ones who are not confident they can deliver the exceptional customer service that you want to deliver.

2. Internal. This is where we put more meat on the bones and add in the detail. We take our five promises and detail what actions are needed in order to keep each promise.

For example, the first promise we make in the customer service charter is:

'We will always make you feel welcome'.

From a client perspective, that's great, but from an employee's perspective, it holds no detail. Employees are likely to ask, 'What do I have to do to keep that promise? How do I make them feel welcome?'

We break it down into small manageable actionable chunks.

Establish the brand:

- 'Good morning, welcome to Castledene, John speaking, how can I help you?'
- Let them [the caller] know who they are speaking to

Build trust from the start:

- Personalise the phone call – take and use their [the caller's] name as early as possible

Behaviour breeds behaviour:

- Smile on the phone or face to face
- The customer will know if they are welcome
- Make sure your attitude is contagious and worth catching

If we achieve the above then we will have kept the first promise.

I've detailed our full customer service charter at the end of this module.

Come up with a list

You need a list of promises that you want to make to your customers or clients. Don't make promises that are easy to keep and won't push your business. Make sure they aren't promises that you think you could keep based on current business performance; they need to be promises that you would keep if you had the best business in the world. What's the point in being comfortable? Get out of your comfort zone and think of the service you want to deliver, not what you currently deliver.

A fellow Northerner called Geoff Ramm coined the phrase 'celebrity service'. In his book of the same name, he encourages us to imagine how we treat our current customers and how we would treat George Clooney or Brad Pitt if they walked through the door. Would we give them extra attention? Would we be more attentive, extra chatty, go the extra mile? We should be doing that for all of our customers, not just the famous ones. Geoff raises a great point: aim for celebrity service all of the time.

Of course, when you employ staff, it's impossible to ensure celebrity service all the time. I've had poor service at Virgin, Harrods and John Lewis, and these guys are renowned as the best in their industry. But I've also had celebrity service more often than not from these companies and those isolated instances won't put me off using them. Aim for excellence, and your clients will forgive you the odd blip.

The devil is in the detail

Once you have your list of promises, which can be as few or as many as you want, delve into each promise and come up with a list of actions that, if followed, will achieve the promise. It's no good having high-end promises about customer service, but not knowing whether you can keep them. It's not an easy process and it may take a few sessions to get it right, but it's worth it.

Take, for example, my company promise of:

'We will understand and meet your needs'.

In isolation, how would I know if the company had achieved that promise? I wouldn't; it's hard to quantify. But if I add in some simple rules, such as:

- Never interrupt
- Take detailed notes
- Ask clarifying questions if necessary
- Demonstrate interest – be present
- Always summarise the caller's main points before responding
- Let the caller know the next steps

If we follow all of the above, then along with other details (see end of module), we can say that we *have* understood and met the caller's needs.

That same ethos runs through all of our five promises. Whatever the additional details are, they need to be quantifiable so we will know when we have achieved each promise and hit celebrity service.

Define our company's characteristics – our main characteristic, and this is aligned with our values, is being the best we can be. Always trying to improve. That is at the core of the business and something I'm proud of, and it comes across in the mission statement.

In our mission statement, we are saying we are committed to our staff, customers and community. We won't get to be the best by being anything less than committed. We also have a little phrase written underneath:

'Always striving to be the best we can be'.

Determine what makes our company stand out – this is a little more difficult than the other two points as there are only so many things that can make a company stand out. We wanted to be the complete solution for our customers in not only lettings, which is what we are better known for, but also sales. That was a tall order at the time of rolling the mission statement out as we had only sold investment properties up until then, so it was a bold statement to make.

When will we be the complete sales and lettings solution in the North-East? For Castledene, we have several parameters that need to be achieved in order for us to claim that, but we have those parameters.

When writing your mission statement, make sure that whatever you say is quantifiable and can be measured. It's not just a wishy-washy statement. Unlike your values, your mission statement may need to be regularly updated as your goals may change, maybe because of environmental issues, change of company direction, huge internal issues, or you may have just changed the way you look at business.

Mission statement examples

Have a look at these well-known brands' mission statements. Again, don't copy them; just use them for inspiration.

Look at TED's – 'Spread ideas'. Two words, showing that a mission statement doesn't have to be long.

> To enrich and delight the world through foods and brands that matter.
> **Kellogg Company**

> To give people the power to build community and bring the world closer together.
> **Facebook**

> To create emotional connections with customers around the world through inspiring product design, unique store experiences, and competitive marketing.
> **Gap, Inc**

> To organise the world's information and make it universally accessible and useful.
> **Google**

> To bring inspiration and innovation to every athlete in the world.
> **Nike**

Dedication to the highest quality of Customer Service delivered with a sense of warmth, friendliness, individual pride, and Company Spirit.

Southwest Airlines

To inspire and nurture the human spirit – one person, one cup and one neighborhood at a time.

Starbucks

To grow a profitable airline, that people love to fly and where people love to work.

Virgin Atlantic

To be the global leader in the sporting goods industry with brands built on a passion for sports and a sporting lifestyle.

Adidas

Our vision is to be Earth's most customer-centric company; to build a place where people can come to find and discover anything they might want to buy online.

Amazon

Castledene customer service charter

Promise 1 – *we will always make you feel welcome.*

Establish the brand:

- 'Good morning, welcome to Castledene, John speaking, how can I help you?'
- Let them [the caller] know who they are speaking to

Build trust from the start:

- Personalise the phone call – take and use their [the caller's] name as early as possible

Behaviour breeds behaviour:

- Smile on the phone or face to face
- The customer will know if they are welcome
- Make sure your attitude is contagious and worth catching

Promise 2 – *we will understand and meet your needs.*

Actively listen to what the caller is saying:

- Never interrupt
- Take detailed notes
- Ask clarifying questions if necessary
- Demonstrate interest – be present
- Always summarise the caller's main points before responding
- Let the caller know the next steps

Establish an emotional connection:

- Put yourself in their shoes
- Be empathetic *not* sympathetic

The customer should never have to ask twice.

Never over promise *but* over deliver

Promise 3 – *we will build relationships through professionalism and trust.*

We build trust by having integrity – we do what we say when we say we will do it.

The customer will always know what we will be doing next and by when.

Leave the customer with a positive phrase:

- It's been a pleasure speaking with you today
- I'm happy that we resolved your issue

Give the customer an opportunity to cover anything else:

- Is there anything you would like to discuss today?

Promise 4 – *we will constantly strive for improvements through innovative solutions.*

We look to come up with improvements and suggestions and communicate them to management.

We embrace change as it will improve the customer service experience.

If we can make a difference to be more efficient and effective, then we will.

If we are aware of something in the business not performing the way it should be, we will speak to management as non-performance affects the customer service experience.

Promise 5 - *we take pride and enjoyment in what we do.*

- We complete the right actions, first time, every time
- We focus on being a team and making the business better
- We have fun with colleagues and customers without damaging our brand
- We take ownership and accountability for our actions

TASK LIST - VALUES AND BELIEFS

Imagine - I know it's a morbid thought - how you would want to be remembered. Would you want people to say he/she was an honest person or they had integrity or they would help anyone?

- What do you hold close to you? Community, family, being the best?
- Have a look at the common values listed below and see which are important to you. Don't pick the ones you think or feel you should have - make sure you truly believe in them. If you are not keen on the word but agree with the sentiment, use a thesaurus to come up with the word(s) you feel best fit you and your company.

Accountability	Excellence	Perfection
Accuracy	Excitement	Piety
Achievement	Expertise	Positivity
Adventurousness	Exploration	Practicality
Altruism	Expressiveness	Preparedness
Ambition	Fairness	Professionalism
Assertiveness	Faith	Prudence
Balance	Family-orientedness	Quality-orientation
Being the best	Fidelity	Reliability
Belonging	Fitness	Resourcefulness
Boldness	Fluency	Restraint
Calmness	Focus	Results-orientated
Carefulness	Freedom	Rigorous
Challenge	Fun	Security
Cheerfulness	Generosity	Self-actualisation
Clear-mindedness	Goodness	Self-control
Commitment	Grace	Selflessness
Community	Growth	Self-reliance
Compassion	Happiness	Sensitivity
Competitiveness	Hard work	Serenity
Consistency	Health	Service
Contentment	Helping society	Shrewdness
Continuous	Holiness	Simplicity
Improvement	Honesty	Soundness
Contribution	Honour	Speed
Control	Humility	Spontaneity
Co-operation	Independence	Stability
Correctness	Ingenuity	Strategic
Courtesy	Inner harmony	Strength
Creativity	Inquisitiveness	Structure
Curiosity	Insightfulness	Success
Decisiveness	Intelligence	Support
Democraticness	Intellectual status	Teamwork
Dependability	Intuition	Temperance
Determination	Joy	Thankfulness
Devoutness	Justice	Thoroughness
Diligence	Leadership	Thoughtfulness
Discipline	Legacy	Timeliness
Discretion	Love	Tolerance
Diversity	Loyalty	Traditionalism
Dynamism	Making a difference	Trustworthiness
Economy	Mastery	Truth-seeking
Effectiveness	Merit	Understanding
Efficiency	Obedience	Uniqueness
Elegance	Openness	Unity
Empathy	Order	Usefulness
Enjoyment	Originality	Vision
Enthusiasm	Patriotism	Vitality
Equality		

TASK LIST – MISSION STATEMENT

- What does your business do for your customer? What is it that's unique?
- What are your company's style and characteristics?
- What words or phrases do you use?
- What is your ultimate mission?
- What has to happen for you to be happy with what you have achieved?
- Is it big enough for you to take an amount of time to achieve it?
- How will you know if you have achieved your mission?

TASK LIST – CUSTOMER SERVICE PROMISE

- Write down a list of promises that you want to deliver for your customers
- Make it specific to customer service
- Write down sub actions that you need to achieve in order for you to keep those promises
- Keep it between four and seven promises

TWO

RECRUITMENT

The recruitment process is one of the most highly debated topics in all of business, but why? It boils down to the fact that if we get it wrong, it can cost us a lot.

A report carried out in 2017 by the Recruitment and Employment Confederation stated:

- 85% of human resources (HR) decision makers admit their organisation has made a bad hire, but a third (33%) believe that these mistakes cost their business nothing
- A poor hire at mid-manager level with a salary of £42,000 can cost a business more than £132,000
- The hidden costs involved in bad recruitment include money wasted on training, lost productivity, and increased staff turnover
- Four in ten employers (39%) admit that the interviewing and assessment skills of their staff should be improved

The cost of poor recruitment is high for UK businesses, and is not only measured in monetary terms, but also resources such as time, lost productivity and – in my opinion the most costly of all – team culture.

Team culture is vital to a well-run business. Getting the right people working for your organisation, all giving their best, is essential to its success. The wrong employee lays waste to success and can set you back months in terms of culture and attitude. When the wrong employee stays longer than they should in your organisation, it sends messages out to the rest of the staff and can set precedents in the business.

Recruitment questions to ask yourself

Do I need to recruit?

It sounds a bit of a silly question, but it isn't. The bigger some companies get, the more they get into the mentality that they just need to throw bodies at a problem or an issue, but that isn't always the case. I've made the same mistake when I thought I needed to recruit, recruit, recruit.

Can the process be automated or outsourced? This should be the first question you ask yourself as a business leader. Do you really need to recruit someone for this issue or problem? Just because someone has left or handed in their notice, it doesn't necessarily mean they need to be replaced.

I'll give you an example – in one of my company's branches, four people managed around 400 properties. At 100 properties per person, this is pretty standard for the industry, maybe even slightly on the low side.

My team and I looked at the bottlenecks in the business. Who was doing what, how could we make the process simpler? And in the end, when one of the four moved on to another company, we didn't replace them. We sat the remaining three employees down and showed them that they still had the same amount of time to manage a few more properties. Over a period of time, we had slowly implemented efficiencies, so while it may have felt to them as if we were dumping a load of work on them, we had equipped them with the tools and skills to be more efficient with their time.

It's not always about throwing staff at an issue. Be smart. Having said that, there may be times when you have a genuine recruitment issue.

Where to go to recruit

Once you have identified that you have a real recruitment need, then you need to look for staff – but where do you go? The good news is that there are lots of ways to get your advert to the masses.

Recruitment companies. At Castledene, we have links with a few trusted recruitment agencies that give us preferential rates because we use them all the time and put a lot of business their way through referrals. The advantage of using these companies is that they screen most of the unsuitable CVs and only send us the good ones – well, that's the theory. The downside is that they are expensive, and at first we need to educate the recruiter as to what we are looking for. Which is fine as we only get out of something

45

what we put into it.

Job sites. We also advertise on Indeed and similar websites, which most potential candidates are constantly monitoring. It's easy and cheap to put an advert on these sites.

Facebook. Love it or loathe it, Facebook is a huge resource to tap in to. We always advertise our vacancies on Facebook. In all honesty, the results we get aren't as good as when we advertise on websites like Indeed, but it's cheap, we have had good results, and it builds great brand awareness.

Current staff. We offer a £250 referral fee to any member of staff who puts us in touch with somebody we end up employing. That's a great way of getting people to put forward people they know, and they won't put a poor-quality candidate forward as it would reflect badly on them.

There will be many more options than the above suggestions, but these are the ones that work for us. One thing to remember is that good staff are like buses: no decent candidates come along for ages, then all of a sudden a few arrive at the same time. Don't worry about recruitment – it's the same as most things in business and in life. If you do the little things consistently well, then the big things will work out naturally.

competent, but would you invest every penny of the family fortune with him? Of course not. That's down to his values, or lack of them.

How to discover someone's values

The interview stage is the perfect time to discover the candidate's values to see if you can work with them, but how do you do this? How do you get the person to open up?

If I'm honest, there is no hard and fast way to do it, but by following a few basic steps, you will be right about 95% of the time, which is how often we get it right at Castledene. Compare that to around 50/50 when we first started – it's a huge improvement.

Get your values nailed

I won't go into too much detail on values as we covered them in the previous chapter. Suffice to say you need to have absolutely first-class values rolled out across the business so everyone is aware of them. Everyone needs to sign up to them and follow them in every decision or action they make.

Ask for stories or long examples

How we lie is not complicated. To lie, we need to have a great imagination as we must construct an alternative reality where the lie actually happened, so it appears real. When we're put on the spot with a closed question, where the answer will be a yes or no, we don't have to think much. Some people then just deny things without even thinking them through.

In an interview, when you ask candidates to give examples of when they dealt with a particular situation or tell you a story about it, if they're going to lie, then their brain has to construct a brand-new memory, which is more difficult than you may think, especially in a relatively stressful situation such as a job interview.

At Castledene, we make the interview process formal and, if I'm honest, slightly uncomfortable. It's not exactly the Spanish Inquisition or the KGB, but we want our candidates to demonstrate that they can handle pressure.

Depending on the job you are recruiting for, ask yourself whether you want the candidates to be able to handle stressful situations. Do you really want a manager who crumbles under pressure if a landlord or vendor asks a question? Of course not.

Ask for stories that will show a candidate's values and whether they align with your company values. For example, our values at Castledene are 'Be better', and in the interview we ask several questions centred around examples or stories of being better or progressing. We basically ask the same question a few times, but it's worded differently each time. If we get the same story, but the details have changed, then we know the candidate is exaggerating or making it up.

Have a set list of questions

It stands to reason that you need to have a robust interview process, but you may be surprised how many people go into interviewing candidates without any structure. As a result, they shouldn't be surprised when new recruits don't work out.

Have you ever said to yourself, 'I should have given the job to the other guy,' or 'The first lady was actually a better fit'? If you have doubts about the candidate you select, your recruitment process is almost certainly flawed.

Staff don't work out, it's a fact of life and business. Some people are great at interviews and some are pretty poor, but getting a process in place really reduces the possibility of the poor hires. When you interview people, you need to be able to compare and contrast them against each other in a fair and balanced way to make sure you recruit the best of the pool of talent. If you wing it or have different processes for different people, then you are not comparing apples with apples.

Whatever questions you have, use the same ones for everyone and score candidates out of five or ten, depending on what you feel comfortable with. That way, over the course of the interviews, you will be able to count up the score and get a pretty accurate idea of the top few candidates.

It's a proven fact that if we are interviewing all day, we will automatically score the people we interview at the end of the day lower than the ones we saw at the start of the day, regardless of how good they are. We are fresher and more interested in the morning, whereas in the late afternoon or evening, we're likely to be tiring of the process. It's no one's fault – it's just the way our brains work. This makes having a fair and balanced way of comparing the candidates with each other even more relevant.

Stick to the script

I don't mean you need to be robotic, but you do need to be efficient and effective when interviewing people. Interviewing is time consuming, so you need a system – what to say to pull the conversation back when it inevitably goes off course, how to dig deep for more information, etc. These are issues an interviewer will face – I've held interviews when I've politely asked what the candidate does for fun and have endured a fifteen-minute explanation of line dancing. I'm not joking, either. At the time, I was young and inexperienced, so instead of butting in and saying, 'Great, thanks for that, moving on… ' I just sat there nodding and listening, pretending to be interested, which made them talk even more passionately.

Using phrases such as 'Thanks for that' or 'Great, that's all I wanted to know' or 'Moving on' or any combination of these, you can pull the conversation back on track. Time is precious, so don't waste it.

Should you talk about your company?

At Castledene, we always start the conversation, after thanking the candidate for coming in, by asking them, 'What do you know about the company?' I personally think it speaks volumes if someone has gone out of their way to research the company; it's a huge tick in their box.

We then go on to tell them what we are looking for, what the job opportunity is and where it fits into the big picture. That takes about five to ten minutes, and then we get started with the traditional interview process.

The reason we talk about ourselves first is that we are setting expectations. I don't want candidates to blabber on in the interview, get to the end, hear about our plans and the role, and say, 'Oh, this doesn't sound right for me.' It's far better to get it out of the way at the beginning.

We have had a few occasions where, after we have told the candidate about the role, what we expect, salary, etc, they have said, 'The wage is too low,' or 'I didn't think the role was going to be like that.' Then they leave, which saves us forty minutes to an hour of wasting our time.

Remember in an interview that you are selling yourself and the company to the candidate. It's definitely a two-way process – you want to impress the right candidate so that they want to come and work for you. It's a crowded marketplace out there, so there aren't dozens of highly motivated and accountable property staff just waiting for your call.

The job offer

You have found your perfect candidate and you want to offer them the job. Always phone them up to make the offer and have a chat, sending the job offer pack to them as quickly as possible.

A job offer pack needs to consist of three things: the job offer letter, the contract and the job description. That's all you need to send the successful candidate. Don't over complicate things; keep it simple. If they have any questions, invite them to get in touch with you as soon as possible so there will be no hold ups with their employment.

We get in touch with our successful candidates once a week to make sure everything is OK and they are still motivated and looking forward to working with us. Leaving one employer to go to another, or starting out in or re-entering the workplace, can be an emotional and nervous time for some people, so be empathetic. It says a lot about you and your management style.

The fall through

When you are in business, you will inevitably have people who say they want to work for you, accept the job offer, then at the last minute decide to stay in their current employment. It is frustrating, but there's nothing much you can do about it. It has happened to my company on a number of occasions and it's mostly down to two reasons:

- Better the devil you know – it's too much of a leap for the candidate to take. They may have been working for their employer for a number of years and it's safe; it's what they know.
- They used our job offer as leverage – they went back to their employer and said, 'I've been offered another job, but if you pay me £3,000 a year more, then I'll stay.' This is the one that really aggravates me as the candidate clearly had no intention of leaving their current employer and has wasted our time.

All we do when this happens is put the candidate on a 'No interview' list. Regardless of how many times they respond to our future adverts, we never give them an interview. You may be surprised at the amount of times these types of people will reapply for jobs with a company they have let down in the past.

The first day

The first day in a new job is a bit like the first day at school, so it's imperative that the new staff member receives the best possible welcome. I'm not suggesting that you roll out the red carpet, but you must ensure they have everything they need to start the role ready prepared: relevant email addresses, PC, work station, etc.

You then start the job of training and development, but what does that look like?

Our induction training only takes about half a day. We cover the generic stuff like health and safety, who's who in the business, how Castledene started, etc, then we hand the new recruit a copy of the training matrix and go through it with them. We want to get their opinion of what they are strong at and what needs further development. That way we have a list of their strengths and weaknesses from day one so we can tailor the training. For example, if they say they are not great at rent arrears chasing, then we can focus on that for longer when it comes up in the training.

Of course, we also go through the operational side of the new recruit's job role, spending half a day on the training, then the remainder of the day asking them to implement what they have learned. The vast majority of people respond better to doing the action rather than learning the theory.

The first thirty days

Depending on your training programme, you are likely to have rolled out the main bulk of it within the first month. Touch base with the new recruit or their line manager every day, seeing how they are getting on. Is there anything you need to do to help them?

At the end of each week, our managers sit down with the new starter in a formal way and spend 10 minutes giving the new starter some feedback. At the thirty-day mark, we have a one to one with the new starter and go over the training matrix we asked them to complete on day one. The beauty of this is that we will now have a month's worth of evidence to agree or disagree with the way the employee scored themselves. For example, if they scored themselves a four for customer service, which is exceeding expectations, and we think they are really a three, we can give reasons for this. What this does is focus us on the development areas of the employee, so rather than offering blanket training for training's sake, we can now have more of a targeted and efficient approach for both the company and the new employee. As you can probably tell by now, I hate wasting time in anything I do.

The first ninety days

The ninety-day mark is more often than not the end of the probation period. If you have followed all the actions I've suggested in this chapter, you will massively increase the chances of the employee working out with a permanent contract.

At this stage, you sit down with the employee and go over all the good points and all the issues you have with them. You will have all the information to hand from the training matrix and the monthly one to ones, so none of it should come as a surprise to the employee. It's just reiterating everything they have already been told.

You have three options at this stage:

- It's not working out and you need to part ways
- You extend the probation as there are a few things that need working on
- The new recruit passes their probation and you offer them full-time employment

The first and last are easier to implement than the middle one, but don't feel as though you can't extend the recruit's probationary period. That's what it's there for. If you are not sure, then extend it for another three months – nothing wrong with that, as long as you explain why you are extending it, what issues you have and how the recruit can improve. If they do improve, then there will be a full-time contract waiting for them.

After the ninety days

Now you are up and running, as the saying goes. Constant communication and support are vital to ensuring the success of new staff. Without either, you are reducing their chances of working out. A little bit of effort up front from you or you managers will pay dividends in the long term.

Staff are an investment and need to be nurtured as such. Put the effort in early and you will reap the rewards later – in every case where we at Castledene have done this, the staff member has paid us back. And being completely honest, when we haven't put the effort in, they have struggled, and that wasn't their fault. That was our failing.

Don't make the same mistake – put the ideas in this chapter into practice and give your recruitment process and your new staff members the best chance of success.

TASK LIST – RECRUITMENT

- Design your ideal recruitment process
  - Where will you put the adverts?
  - How will you advertise, what language will you use, and how will you make your vacancy stand out?
- Understand what the company values and beliefs are
- Set out your list of questions
- Score the candidates based on their answers – be fair and equitable with all the candidates
- Know what you want to get across about the role or the company, but don't talk too much, as tempting as that may be
- When you're offering the successful candidate the job, do it as efficiently and effectively as possible
- Have a plan for when they start and see it through

THREE

HOW TO SYSTEMISE THE BUSINESS

For this module, I've reprinted parts from my Amazon best-selling book *From Stress To Success*. Why reinvent the wheel? It was written to break down how to systemise your business.

Many people think that you can systemise a business simply by writing a manual. Nothing could be further from the truth. The manual is the basis for the systemisation process, but it's only 20% of the process. Having said that, it is the part that takes the longest to get right. You need to get it as complete as you can, right from the start.

The operations manual

The operations manual is like the cornerstone of a building or the engine of a car. Without it, the rest of the process is a waste of time and energy. When I wrote my first operations manual years ago, I was jumping for joy. It was my first step to business freedom. Even though it was only twenty pages long and full of spelling mistakes, it showed me I was heading in the right direction.

When you're writing your operations manual, be aware that you won't get it right first time. It's a huge step in the right direction, but some of your employees won't thank you for it. Persistence and consistency are the keys here. If employees show resistance and pick holes in your manual, that's to be expected. It happened to me and it has happened to everyone who's consulted with me. People don't like change, especially long-serving staff, so don't be surprised if they are wary of the operations manual. They might worry that the aim of the manual is to make them redundant. In fact, nothing could be further from the truth – the only person it aims to make redundant is you.

Remember, not everyone will make the journey with you. This move towards systemising your business may polarise opinion. Some people will thrive on it as it will be the change they have been waiting for. Others will resent it and will look for new jobs, as their performance can now be measured, highlighted and managed accordingly. These are the ones who have probably not been performing to the best of their ability while you and your other employees have been slogging your guts out, blissfully unaware that you've been covering for them.

If you employ good friends, partners or family, introducing changes may lead to arguments in your personal life. Working with people you have a relationship with outside work can be difficult, and separating the two worlds is impossible for some.

The question you need to ask yourself is this: 'Does my personal relationship with this person/these people mean more to me than my business and my family's future?' If the answer is yes, you don't need to read any more of this book, as systemising your business is not for you. But if you want great company performance, a saleable asset and the option to retire, and you want to bring your family and friends along with you, carry on reading.

As with most things, it's not what you say, it's how you say it. Telling your staff what you intend to do and how you're going about it can make all the difference. If you say, 'I'm systemising the business, so it's my way or the highway', expect friction and anger. But if you're genuine and explain that the manual is there to help everyone, to make their jobs easier and more efficient, and to benefit the customer, you'll get a better response.

Plan what you are going to say to your employees. Never just send an email – it's impersonal and it doesn't give people the chance to ask questions. Make sure everyone understands what's going to happen. Communicate with them at every point along the way. Business decisions that demand co-operation from staff at all levels deserve nothing less than effective communication.

What is the operations manual?

The operations manual is the company bible. We call ours the *Castledene Way*, and if something isn't in it, we don't do it.

Your manual needs to set out everything about your business, from how to operate machinery to how you interact with customers, to how you report your results, to what you do when things go wrong. If something happens in your business that isn't in your manual, your manual is not complete.

Going back to the car analogy, you could have the best car in the world on your drive (the Aston Martin DB7, by the way), but if it's missing a front tyre, it's just a piece of metal. It isn't fit for the purpose it was designed for. This is the same as not having a complete operations manual. If there are gaps, according to Murphy's law, whatever is missing from the manual will go wrong. People don't like mistakes – we want things to be perfect as quickly as possible. But perfection takes time. If you're going to systemise your business, you need to be prepared to put in the hours at the beginning to reap the rewards at the end. I assure you, it's worth it.

Should your procedures simply detail what you do? Of course not, because what you do might not be the best way of doing it. If you already have a business, you need to go back to basics. If you're just starting one, you haven't yet got into the habit of running your business in a certain way, so you need to work on your business rather than in it.

Imagine looking down on your business as if you're looking down on a patient on the operating table. Sometimes you won't like what you see, but brutal honesty is your friend. Anything less is not doing you, your staff, your business or your customers any favours.

Take another analogy: I love my children with all my heart, but I don't look at them through rose-tinted glasses. If they mess up, I tell them. If they're naughty, I don't pacify them with a treat. To prepare them for the real world, I treat them with honesty. This is how you need to look at the current way you run your business. If things aren't working well in a particular part of the business, recognise that. If certain members of staff aren't pulling their weight, that needs to be documented too. The aim of the manual is to help you be the best you can be – anything less is cheating.

Although I've never met you and I don't know what you do, I know you're not running your business as efficiently or effectively as possible. How do I know this? It's simple – no business runs at 100% all the time. It's impossible. People don't perform, machinery breaks down and automation fails. It's how you deal with these issues that determines how successful you are.

When you're writing your manual, on the one hand you need to write down what you do, but on the other hand you need to ignore what you do. Confused? Let me explain.

First, take into account your company core values and your mission statement. They may be bold and ambitious, but remember, 'go big or go home'. These documents will keep you on the right track when you're writing your manual.

Second, write the manual with the end user in mind. By end user, I don't mean your staff, who will be the ones reading, using and implementing the procedures. I mean the customer who will use your product or service. Make sure your values and beliefs shine through the procedures in your operations manual. Everything in your manual must revolve round the customer.

I don't subscribe to the belief that the customer is always right, or even often right. Some people just like to moan, and you can't please everyone all the time. Not everyone likes Nike, Apple or Aston Martin, but these are leading brands in their industries.

I subscribe to Ken Blanchard's idea of having 'raving fans', not customers. Raving fans are the people who receive such good customer service from you that they want to shout about how good you are. For example, our ordinary customers will just say, 'Oh yes, I use Castledene to manage my properties', but our fans tell everybody at every opportunity why they love working with us. Because of them, we get a large number of referrals and repeat business.

Writing your operations manual is your opportunity to make your service better and more customer-focused. The broad brush strokes of what you do may be the same, but by tweaking the details, you can improve the service. Orienting your manual to customer service won't put an end to complaints – remember, you can't please all the people all the time, so write your manual with the majority in mind.

Never be tempted to fit the procedures in your operations manual around your staff. I have seen businesses make this mistake countless times. Never compromise on customer service because of a staffing inefficiency or an employee's lack of knowledge. Instead, invest time and effort in training or move employees around so everything's covered. Do you think your customer cares that Robert only works three days a week or Mary doesn't know how to use the software? Of course not, so don't put yourself or your business in that position.

Your operations manual is your chance to make your business super-efficient, but remember that it has to be realistic. It's no good writing procedures that you have no chance of following. Remember, superior customer service is the key.

The art of delegation – make yourself redundant

When you're writing your operations manual, your ultimate goal is to make yourself redundant. This might seem alien if you've worked hard for years and you're proud to have done so, but this is a unique situation. You need to make it possible for the business to operate as efficiently as it can without you. One of the most important reasons to systemise your business is that it gives you a saleable asset. You might never sell your business or pass it on to your children, but at least you'll have the option to do so if you wish.

The most important of all reasons to systemise is that it gives you options – options to spend more time with your family and make sure they never have to go through hard times.

The excuses

There are two types of people in the world – those who do things and those who make excuses. Believe me, I've heard them all from people I've worked with. Ultimately, whether you delegate is down to you and your desire to change your life.

Here are the two most common excuses in my experience:

No one can do it as well as I can. If this is your excuse, either you have too high an opinion of yourself or your employees are not up to the task. If the problem is your staff, you have two options. You can either invest time and effort in upskilling people so they can perform the tasks to the required standard, or you can recruit people who are better skilled and more competent.

I know I'm not the best person at my job – and if I can accept that, you can too. That means there are people out there you can subcontract to or delegate to. What's important is to be able to see people's potential and let go.

I don't have the time to train the staff. The brutally honest answer to this excuse is that you need to make time. You can't do anything worthwhile overnight – it takes hard work, dedication and persistence. So if you want to achieve the end goal, you need to put in the hard graft. We will go over some tips on how to break down the training process later.

Who can I delegate to?

The first question you need to ask yourself is whether a task should be delegated internally or externally. Here's how this worked for me.

When I started the company, I did everything myself: the accounts, the viewings, meeting the landlords, the internal paperwork and much more. I had two members of staff who worked hard and did what I asked of them, but without good systems, there was no real consistency and stability to anything we did.

When I first systemised the business, I looked at all the jobs I was doing and identified which income-generating tasks I could delegate internally or externally. I was surprised by how many tasks I could easily pass to someone else. I delegated the accounts to a local accountant, who not only did a much better job than I could, but also made the process of recording invoices and receipts much more efficient. It paid for itself from day one, as I was spending no time at all on accounts. Remember, your time has value, so value it.

I managed to delegate the viewings to one member of staff, who thrived on it and did a brilliant job. I also employed an additional person to manage a portfolio of properties that I had been managing. This freed up huge amounts of my time.

I enjoyed and was good at getting business in, so I continued to do that. As soon as my workload increased and resources allowed, I delegated more tasks to free up more of my time to continue working on income-generating tasks.

After a few years, I was in the position where almost any task in the business could be delegated to internal employees. This included training, audits, HR, setting targets and recruitment. I now don't get involved in anything to do with running the business. I could retire tomorrow if I wanted to, but I love what I do and I still have a passion for growing the business.

Look at each task in your business. Could you give it to someone internally? With the right training, would they be capable of completing the task to the company's high standard? Or can you delegate it, like I did with the accounting, to an external professional? There's a cost involved in delegating, and I appreciate that when you're starting out things can be tight in the finance department, but the time and effort you'll save by delegating means you'll be free to perform the tasks that bring in the income.

When I first bought properties, I refurbished them myself because I thought it would save time and money. I did save money on each particular job, but overall it was a terrible decision for the business. I missed out on countless deals with estate agents because I was too busy stripping wallpaper or knocking down walls. Eventually I learned that getting someone else in to do the work not only resulted in a better standard of refurbishment, but also freed me up to visit the estate agents and look for the next deal.

It's a false economy to think you'll save money by doing everything yourself. In the long run, you'll miss out on opportunities that could have made you much more money.

Whether you can delegate enough tasks to make yourself redundant will depend on where you are in the business process. If you're just starting out, you may have to do many of the tasks yourself and delegating might not always be possible. But it's still important to take a long, hard look at all the tasks you're doing to see if you really do have to do them yourself, or if you can pass them to someone else.

Delegation is an art, not a science. It takes time to let go. You need the right people in the right areas of the business, supporting you in the right way. You also need people who buy in to your business vision and beliefs. Have frank conversations with people you want to delegate to – especially if they don't work directly for you, as you'll have less control over how they represent your business. Don't see this as a reason not to work with them, though. Instead, use it as a starting point for the conversation. Explain what you need from them and set the expectations from the beginning. Delegate at the earliest opportunity.

A top tip is to write a list of everything you do, including the amount of time it takes you to carry out that particular action.

Next to each item, write the name of someone in the business who could take on this task, or someone it could be delegated to externally. Ensure the people you want to delegate to have the skills or the resources to upskill themselves to take on the additional tasks successfully. You may well be surprised at how much you can delegate.

Auditing

Auditing is *essential* to ensuring that systemisation works. Without it, no matter how good your operations manual or how great your training and development is, you'll move backwards, and mistakes will happen and go unchecked. An audit gives you confidence that your procedures are working, and your employees are performing as the business requires.

In our daily lives, we audit pretty much everything – it's second nature. Every time we have the car washed, we inspect it to make sure nothing has been missed. When the online food shopping arrives, we check the items off against the order list. Every time we go shopping for clothes, we see whether they fit and whether they have any defects. We were all audited at school by the exams at the end of term. We audit and are audited in every part of our personal lives, so why should auditing in business be any different?

In my experience, few businesses audit. This is shocking. How do the owners know if their employees are making mistakes? Not everyone will complain when they receive poor service; not everyone brings it to the attention of the manager.

You can only imagine the number of times I've heard people say after a negative review or a complaint, 'If only I'd known so-and-so was doing this,' or 'If only I'd known so-and-so hadn't done that.' If they had audited their business, they would have had a good chance of picking up on the mistake sooner. Will an audit pick up every mistake a member of staff ever makes? Of course not. What it will do is change the culture of the business from an attitude of 'That'll do' to 'I'm going to do this as well as I can.'

Landlords my team and I work with sometimes tell us that they decided to change letting agents because the previous agent gave them poor service. When we take over a property from another agent, we ask for the property file. This should contain various pieces of information, some required by law and others that are simply best industry practice. I've yet to see a file that I'm truly impressed with. Unfortunately, in many cases I have to break the news to the landlord that they haven't been legally covered for certain things. I don't believe for one second that the previous agent didn't know they had to meet certain legal requirements; I believe they didn't have the right processes in place, and they didn't audit to ensure their services and procedures were consistent.

When Castledene loses properties (yes, we do lose properties), we want the agent taking over to be amazed by how good our files are.

Sounds a bit cheesy? Not in the slightest – we take pride in our work and we want other agents to be impressed.

This consistency is only possible with regular and intense audits, ensuring the same high quality of paperwork every time. It's human nature to slack off when we know we're not being watched. I do this myself. If I go to the gym on my own, I don't always lift the heaviest weights I can and I might not do as many sets – and this is coming from someone who played sport professionally and loves the gym. A good procedural audit in a business shouts out, 'If you slack off, you'll be found out.'

It takes time and effort to get complete buy in from staff, but once you've done that, people even start looking forward to the auditing process. For example, in my business, the audit plays a big part in which branch is chosen as branch of the month. This motivates employees to put forward their files to the area manager rather than hiding them away and hoping they won't be picked. It's great to see that our employees are proud of their work and want to be noticed for it.

Employees may see auditing as Big Brother watching them, and some members of staff will think you're doing it to check up on them. Let's be honest: you are. Remember, you want the business to be the best it can be and you want to give your employees the chance to be the best versions of themselves, so why not give them the best tools?

Auditing is a way of helping people improve. By identifying their weaknesses, you can provide training and development in certain areas so they can do better. I got buy in from my staff by explaining that I wanted the company to be the best and not apologising for that. They understood this. I then explained that to be the best, we needed to understand where we were weakest. By doing so, we could improve our processes and procedures to ensure that all employees and the company became the best in the UK. I also said that although we would highlight some basic issues with employees' work and the procedures, with time and training, we would all improve and grow together.

Why audit?

You need to audit for the following reasons:

To achieve management priorities. Businesses move quickly and priorities change. Auditing the business can align management priorities with operational priorities.

For example, a few years ago, my team and I changed how we managed some of our branches, placing much more emphasis on data and KPIs. Operationally it wasn't a huge task, but the change in mind-set that managers had to make certainly was. We became, and still are, a results-based company. We began setting targets for managers, and KPIs formed a big part of that. This works well for audits, as it takes the emotion out of the process and focuses on the facts: either you achieve your targets, or you don't.

To meet the requirements of management systems, regulations, contracts and the law. This is especially relevant in the property industry, where there are frequent regulatory and legislative changes. It can be worrying to work in an industry where the threat of legal action is all too common. An audit checks whether you have adapted your procedures to comply with any changes and whether your employees are keeping to those changes.

To meet the requirements for evaluating suppliers. If you use suppliers in any shape or form, you need to know if they are performing to your standards. Their work may affect your reputation and brand, so it's essential that you only work with people you trust and who share your vision and values.

This is easier said than done. Contractors often start off well, but get complacent and perform less well over time. Auditing can keep contractors and suppliers on their toes and make them think twice about cutting corners. It won't catch every problem, but it will pick up on most. This could be seen as trying to catch suppliers out, but if you blindly trust that everything is going to be fine and you don't audit them, you're asking for trouble.

To meet customer requirements. Different customers will have different needs. In my opinion, great customer service is about finding out what your customers' needs and motivations are and meeting them on an individual basis. Of course, you can't bend over backwards for every customer, but you can tailor your service to suit them.

Taking my own business as an example, while most landlords we work with want us to pay their portion of the rent as soon as we receive it from tenants, a few want us to hold on to the rent until the start of the month. We audit the business to check that we have tailored our services and we have met customers' needs.

To assess risks to the organisation. An audit not only aligns well with legislative requirements, it also takes into account other risks to the business, such as theft and fraud.

For example, one of my former branch managers stole from the company. How did my team and I find out even though the head office was 100 miles away? It was all down to KPIs and audits. The KPIs highlighted an anomaly in the financial takings. We immediately carried out an impromptu audit and discovered some money had been taken. All this happened in three days.

Just imagine if we hadn't had the KPIs and auditing process in place – how long could the manager have done this for and how many customers would have had their money stolen? My company would have suffered terrible damage to its reputation. Thanks to the audit, every penny was recovered, and no one lost out.

Review – work out what or who to fix

Based on the results of your internal audit, you'll need to carry out a review. Believe me, you will find something in the audit process, especially as your company gets bigger. I was taught that if you can't find something in the audit, that says more about you as an auditor than it does about the company. It doesn't mean that your company is outstanding and has done everything completely correctly – it means that you haven't done your audit thoroughly enough to find the non-conformances.

The good news is that you don't need to worry when you do find issues. If you have the mind-set that you're always striving to improve your company, issues that come up in an audit are nuggets of continuous improvement. The benefit of having a structured review process that's linked to feedback is that you can always have a plan to improve the situation. The purpose of a review is to see where and how you can move forward. Without this part of the process, you'll just keep making the same mistakes, which helps no one. Continual improvement is the key to a successful business, so always strive to move forward.

Sometimes, as a business owner, you can find it hard to review people you have recruited or processes you have implemented. I'll be honest – when I started reviewing my businesses, I found several problems that stemmed from things that I had initiated. It was difficult to admit that something I'd put in place had never really worked. As soon as I got over my ego, I recognised that I shouldn't view this as a failure, but as a step towards finding a better process. After that, I felt much better about reviewing people I had employed or procedures I had written.

In my company, I reached the stage a few years ago where my team reviews the people and processes. This makes everything much easier and more efficient for me. This will happen to you too: the larger your organisation becomes, the less time you'll be spending 'pulling out the weeds'. Your employees will drive continual improvement forward for you, and the review process is integral to this.

Person or process?

There are two main types of issues in a business: people issues and process issues. As a reviewer, it's your job to use the facts and evidence to determine who or what is at fault and identify the right course of action to prevent an issue happening again.

The main objective of systemisation is the continuous improvement of the business. Be aware that, depending on your findings, you may need to be brutally honest: people may lose their jobs, departments may be closed and projects may be shelved. While the immediate action that comes out of the review may seem negative, the overarching strategic goal is to improve the company and keep it moving forward. That, in itself, is positive.

Be mindful of the reason for or the root cause of the issue. On the face of it, it could look as if an employee is not achieving what's expected of them or is involved in the same issue again and again. Some people will assume that this is a people issue and the employee needs to be more motivated or learn new skills. Some may even say that the employee needs performance management or that their employment should be terminated. This is a knee-jerk reaction. You need to use what the academics call critical analysis to understand the whole issue and find its root cause.

Root-cause analysis

I've heard this being called investigation analysis and failure analysis, among other things, but they are all essentially the same. To analyse the root cause, you need to ask three questions:

- What's the issue or problem?
- Why did it happen (what caused it)?
- What do you need to do to stop it happening again?

Without going too far into root-cause analysis and problem-solving, which is a book in itself, I will share a simple but effective technique that I use. I've never come across a problem that this technique has not been able to help me solve.

The five whys

This technique was first used by Sakichi Toyoda, one of the founders of the Japanese industrial revolution. Although he developed the technique back in the 1930s, it became popular in the 1970s, and Toyota still uses it today. I use it a lot in my businesses with great effect.

It is basically responding to any answer an employee gives with 'Why?', then asking 'Why?' to their next answer, and the next, and so on. Be as probing as you possibly can be to get to the root cause of the issue.

For example:

You: 'Why didn't you call Mr Smith back?'

Employee: 'I was too busy.'

You: 'Why were you too busy?'

Employee: 'I had to get the report back to accounting by 3pm.'

You: 'Why did you have to get the report back by 3pm?'

Employee: 'That's what we agreed last month in the management meeting.'

You: 'Why did you leave it to the last minute to finish it?'

Employee: 'Don't know... sorry.'

As you can see, by digging deeper, you can uncover the real truth about the situation.

The advantage of the five whys is that it gives a structure for problem-solving while allowing you to focus on the immediate issue at hand. If you've attended senior management or board meetings, you'll know that people start giving opinions that aren't based on facts and quickly meander off the topic. This leads to an unproductive and frustrating meeting. The five whys technique keeps everyone on-topic and forces them to think about a solution to the problem. In my experience, this halves the time needed to resolve the issue. That's a huge amount of time saved, and time is a precious commodity in business.

People quickly get used to the five whys and start looking for solutions to issues before meetings so they have the answers ready. I call this process 'level-up thinking'. You want your staff to think as if they're a level above their role. The portfolio managers think like the branch managers, and the branch managers think like the area manager, and so on. It's a change of mind-set.

CASE STUDY – THE JEFFERSON MEMORIAL

At the Jefferson Memorial in Washington DC, there was a problem. Sparrows were – no other way to say it – defecating all over the memorial. This was making it unpleasant for visitors, many of whom had travelled from all over the world. To make things worse, the excessive water and detergent used to clean up the mess was damaging the monument – so much so that in May 1990, a fifty-pound block of marble fell from it. Luckily, no one was hurt.

Those responsible for the monument wanted to know why they were facing these issues. The report, which allegedly cost nearly two million dollars, was startling.

The birds were attracted to the Jefferson Memorial because of the abundance of spiders – the staple diet for birds. The spiders were attracted to the memorial because of the midges (insects) that were nesting there. The midges were nesting there because of the light. Midges, it turns out, like to procreate in places where the light is just right – and because the lights were turned on at the Jefferson Memorial one hour before dark, it created the kind of mood lighting that midges went crazy for.

How did the authorities resolve the situation? After reviewing the curious chain of events that had led to the problem, and by asking the five whys, they decided to wait until dark before switching on the lights at the Jefferson Memorial. The one-hour delay stopped the midges from congregating around the memorial for some romance. This, in turn, stopped the spiders, which stopped the birds... which sorted out the problem with the droppings.

There is a little more to the story. The park management, although aware of the resolution, tried other methods first because they thought that delaying lighting up the monument would lead to complaints from photographers. They discussed other more expensive solutions, such as hiring more staff to clean the memorial, experimenting with less abrasive cleaning materials or even closing the monument to the public. It took five years and millions of dollars before they accepted the original suggestion.

As you can see from the case study, a simple and cost-saving solution, in the end, was found just by asking a probing question.

Practise the five whys with your team as often as possible so they get used to the technique. This will help you find the best solutions as easily as possible during your review process. It is without doubt the most effective technique I have used for reviewing audits. Everybody knows what they're aiming for and it forces them to dive into the issues. It creates a positive 'no BS' culture in the business.

When to review

The best time to carry out a review of the audit is straight afterwards, when everything is fresh in your mind. No matter how comprehensive your notes, you won't have written everything down, and something, even if it's only small, will get missed if you delay the review. If you wait months or even weeks to look back at your notes, you'll find you won't remember everything. After every audit, discuss the issues and find any solutions necessary.

Who to involve

Like many large companies, Toyota has a 'go and see' policy. This is where the senior decision makers go out on to the shop floor and see processes in action. You can't come up with a solution to a major process issue by sitting in a board room – you need to see how the process really works.

I speak to everybody involved in the process, from the cleaner right through to the finance director if necessary. Everybody's opinions are equally valuable and no suggestion is a silly one. I always thank people for their suggestion. If I don't agree, I explain why. It's good to encourage employees to come forward with possible solutions to issues.

TASK LIST – OPERATIONS MANUAL

- Write down a list of all the basic procedures in your business – a contents list
- Start at the beginning and make it chronological
- Write an idiot's guide to how to do a certain action, carry out a valuation, etc
- Focus on time-bound objectives and who has to do what action
- Audit
- Use the procedures to come up with a list of what needs to be carried out, and use this as a basic audit procedure
- Decide when you will audit certain procedures in your business
- Be unemotional when auditing
- Don't take any excuses – it's either done or it isn't
- Feedback and review

- Give feedback to the appropriate person as soon as possible
- Back it all up with acts or evidence
- Is it a skill or a will issue?
- Decide what you can do to improve before the next audit

FOUR

TRAINING YOUR STAFF

Training your staff is one of the most complex and difficult parts of any business. There have been hundreds of books written on the subject, each with the author's own slant on the latest trend or coaching technique. I've done plenty of research on this topic to find out what works for my business.

Believe me, I've made some mistakes in the way I train my staff. Anyone who's been in business will know that starting and running your own company isn't easy, especially when you're dealing with people. It would be doing you a disservice to claim that everything is wonderful and that I've never made a mistake. I've always learned more from making mistakes than when things have gone smoothly. There's nothing more satisfying than correcting a mistake and finding I've made a good call.

When I started training my staff on systems, embarrassingly, I handed them a twenty-page document and said, 'Learn this.' Believe it or not, I was surprised when things went wrong, but I had to do something about it. And this is where my passion for training and development grew from.

Just dumping a manual on people and expecting them to read it is a more common practice than you may think. What's worrying is when managers or business owners then blame their staff for not learning the material. It's a bit like a teacher handing their pupils a textbook, and then expecting them to pass an exam with flying colours – it's just not going to happen.

We all learn at different paces, and training needs to be tailored to suit the individual. With teaching and learning, one size does not fit all. It never will do: we all have our own strong points and areas where we need further development.

I have researched different learning styles and tests that tell us what our own learning style is. I always thought I was an auditory learner – someone who learns best when they are told something – but a test showed me that in fact, I'm a visual and kinaesthetic learner, which means I need to be shown something and allowed to be hands on. Once I knew this, I realised why I had never retained anything like as much information when I listened to an audiobook as I did when I picked up a book and actually read it.

You can't help how you learn, but you can help how you teach. You have to adapt your various training methods to suit the individual. For my business, I wanted to use a variety of learning applications that would give my staff the best chance to absorb the information. For learning material to be effective, it needs to be consistent with the overall learning objective of the training and development plan – that is, in Castledene's case, to allow employees to be the best that they can be.

As with any training and development in a business, you need to be fully committed to the process and ensure that it isn't a passing phase. It needs to become part of the culture of the business. Everyone, from the managing director to the apprentices, needs to buy in to the company mantra of continual improvement.

Another thing to consider is motivation. What makes people want to come to work and perform to the best of their ability? Is it the money? Is it the promise of extra holidays? Is it to get away from the spouse or the kids?

Motivation has a direct link to not only performance, but also the ability to absorb training. Think about the last time someone spoke to you while you were watching TV. I bet you didn't hear everything they said. That's because you weren't fully motivated to listen to them, so you didn't take in all the information. It's the same with training. Members of staff may turn up, but are they truly present and will they take in the information that you are sharing with them?

The theories on workplace motivation all come down to one thing, although there are many different ways to describe it. Most of us want to be the best we can be. Effective training gives us this opportunity. This leads to a more motivated workforce that performs better, higher levels of customer satisfaction and, eventually, more profit. By motivating staff, you'll get better individual performance, which leads to better company performance. That's part of the systemisation mantra.

I'll cover motivational theory in much more depth in the next chapter.

Which methods work?

The training system I use has evolved a great deal in a few years. I started by giving staff a series of procedures to learn in their own time. Then, I read them out or stood in front of a PowerPoint presentation. Looking back, I realise not only was this soul-destroying, it also gave poor results.

I have since found that the most effective method of training staff on systems is hands-on group involvement or group learning. In the context of systems training, that means me reading through the procedures, and then asking learners to carry out the physical task so they remember it. If we do something often enough, we have a much higher chance of remembering it through repetition.

Most learners won't immediately understand why they have to carry out a certain action as they are not always aware of the bigger picture. Discussing the procedure and explaining why you do certain things and not others makes the process more real and understandable. It also makes people feel that they're a part of the process. During training, members of staff may highlight gaps and make some excellent suggestions. Get them to discuss your procedures, as this gives them the chance to critically analyse ideas and translate them into their own words.

It is possible to cater for the various learning styles by planning a range of activities that include several ways of presenting information. Due to the nature of learning and the complex ways in which we retain information, there are several ways to do this. Asking people to make things, draw things or act out a process will engage the right-hand side of the brain, while asking learners to make lists or create statistical prompts engages the left-hand side of the brain. Role play learning and activity-based groups with a feedback session after the experience are often powerful and effective learning tools because they engage both sides of the brain. When people learn something in a way that suits them, they will come to know it intuitively and understand it intellectually.

People need to be coached in all aspects of their job, not just how to follow procedures. Once you have a robust training and development plan for all staff, monitor it closely against the individual goals of each employee and the strategic goals of the company. It might sound harsh, but if staff goals are not aligned with those of the company, your employees will not perform as you need them to and you will have to decide whether to keep them.

Individual training and development plans

I cannot emphasise enough the importance of having a training and development plan for each employee. This is critical to your company's success and ongoing development.

Each employee plays a vital part in the evolution of a business. If someone doesn't seem to be essential, either they're the wrong employee or their role is not needed. All staff must have a role to play, from the managing director, who is responsible for the strategic direction of the business, to the cleaning staff, who help maintain the brand image by keeping the office hygienic and pleasant. As such, everyone's performance needs to be measured and improved as necessary.

Just for the record, I have an individual training and development plan for myself. Why should I be any different from any other employee? At the time of writing this book, I've just completed a level seven course in leadership and management, and I'm signing up for a master's in leadership and management to take my learning even further.

I do this for a couple of good reasons. Firstly, every time I learn something interesting, I research it and, if applicable, implement it in the business. This has a positive effect, so the company and staff benefit. Secondly, because of the systemisation of the business, I am able to take on a time consuming and difficult course. It's a great feeling to know that I have freed up enough time to learn about my passion, and that what I learn will benefit the company. Learning is part of my job, and the information I learn will make everyone's lives easier and help the company make more money.

Individual training and development plans provide several benefits:

Less management. When you have fully trained and are continuously developing staff, you will spend less time managing them. Some companies believe they haven't got enough time to invest in staff development, but this is short-sighted. A well-trained team that needs less management saves everyone time.

Address employee weaknesses and improve customer service. One of the ultimate goals of your organisation should be to give customers the best possible service. In turn, those customers will recommend you and use your services again. Everyone you employ, including you, has a weakness in some area, and this will have an impact on customer service. Find out what the weaknesses are and adapt the training plan to address them. It will improve customer service and motivate your staff, as it will give them the opportunity to be better versions of themselves.

Consistent performance. Consistency is vital in any organisation. Staff should be performing at the same high level every day. Strong training and development increases consistency in performance. This is especially true when companies are continuously evolving in the pursuit of improvement.

Strong motivation. Most of us want to improve and be the best that we can be. Call it achievement, self-actualisation or whatever you want, but reaching our full potential gives us more motivation to do our job. We want to feel part of the organisation and we want to feel valued. No one wants to feel as though they're just another number going through the motions, so it's important to tailor individual training and development plans to the needs of the learner as well as the needs of the business. I've seen too many generic training plans benefiting half the learners while the other half are ignored.

Increased productivity. If staff have the knowledge to do their job better, more efficiently and to a higher standard, it stands to reason that productivity will increase. How can it not?

The secret to an effective training plan – and, in turn, increased productivity over a sustained period – is that training and learning should be constant. Company leaders tend to train staff on a set of procedures and leave it at that, thinking their responsibility has ended there. That's far removed from what should be happening. Continuous improvement is exactly that – continuous.

Increased profit. In conversations with business owners, I come up against the same argument time and again, which is that it costs money, time and effort to put in place a company-wide training and development plan. These business owners aren't able to see the bigger picture – they're blinkered by the lack of systemisation in their business.

It's a chicken-and-egg situation: as soon as the business is systemised, they'll see the value of training and development, but they haven't got time to get the business to that point. Yes, they will have to invest in the short term, but the rewards in the medium to long term far outweigh the initial outlay.

Reduced cost and wastage. When employees don't perform to their potential, it's usually down to lack of training, especially if poor performance continues over a period of time. Every time a member of staff does something wrong, it needs to be corrected. The employee has to do the task again, someone else has to do it, or even worse, you as the business owner have to do it. This costs the company money and is a waste of time.

Seven steps to developing an effective individual training and development plan

When you're running a business, it's important to ensure that you have the right people in the right roles and that everyone is fully trained, but many companies put training and development low down on the priority list, so they're never going to come up with a specific plan. What's so frustrating is that it isn't even complicated to do.

This section is vital to the ongoing training and development of your staff, and the overall success of systemising your business. The two go hand in hand. Training and development, like the systemisation of the business, is an evolving process. You can't simply write a manual, train employees once and forget about it. You need to review, improve and tweak your plan when needed.

Step 1 - identify goals

To come up with an effective training and development plan, you need to identify the initial goals. This is easier than you might think.

Ask yourself these questions:

- What do I want learners to achieve?
- What's my vision for the training?
- Do my employees need to learn some things before others?
- How will learners know when they have achieved their individual goals?
- What are the company's needs?
- These goals will dictate how you approach the training plan. You need to agree them with your team before the training starts as they are vital to the success of the training plan – it's that simple.

Step 2 - create training materials

This is an extremely important part of the process. As I mentioned earlier, simply handing the staff the procedures to learn or reading them out won't give you the best results, although this has its place alongside other learning materials.

You will have to put some effort and time into creating training materials. Remember to include several types of materials to cater to the different learning styles.

Here are some tips:

- Visual learners – use slides or video
- Auditory learners – use audios and podcasts
- Kinaesthetic learners – people like to feel and touch the material, so include games

Group work can bring out the best in people. It helps them to see other perspectives. Be mindful, though, that some people do not perform well in groups. You will need to make sure that your shy members of staff are not overwhelmed by more extrovert characters in the group.

Take into account the differences in the left and right sides of the brain. Some people are more logical and others are more creative. This affects which type of training they get the most out of.

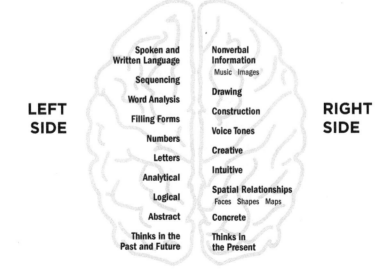

LEFT SIDE

Spoken and Written Language
Sequencing
Word Analysis
Filling Forms
Numbers
Letters
Analytical
Logical
Abstract
Thinks in the Past and Future

RIGHT SIDE

Nonverbal Information
Music Images
Drawing
Construction
Voice Tones
Creative
Intuitive
Spatial Relationships
Faces Shapes Maps
Concrete
Thinks in the Present

Use humour and games and have as much fun as possible. Learners will react better, pay more attention and retain information far more easily if they are having fun than if they feel under pressure or bored.

Step 3 – create a training schedule

Depending on the length of the procedures and what your training goals are, it could take anything from a few weeks to a few months to roll out your procedural training. Bear in mind the following when creating your schedule:

- Don't rush the training. It takes as long as it takes – we all learn at different speeds.
- Don't put too much pressure on new members of staff. If after their probation they have not retained or utilised the information provided through training, you'll need to make a business decision about whether to continue their employment.
- Stick to the training plan. If you miss a session due to workload or some other reason, it sets a precedent for your staff.
- Don't expect learners to understand everything the first time. Plan for additional time so your staff can fully understand a procedure before moving on to the next one.
- If your training material is competent and the matrix is continually completed, you will always know where the

learners are in relation to their training and development plan.

Step 4 – decide who will lead the training

Initially it might be you, the business owner, who carries out the training. I accept that doing all the work yourself seems to go against the grain of this book and the theory of systemisation. In the early days, though, you may have to be all things to all people, depending on your financial resources and time.

If you're carrying out the training, you can't be involved as the person who wrote the systems – you need to put your training hat on. When system designers or authors become heavily involved in the training process, it can lead to disappointment. It's important not to take things to heart if people don't understand the processes. Be open to criticism and suggestions for improvement, which are part of the feedback loop.

If leading training sessions isn't your thing, consider hiring someone to do the job or temporarily delegating the responsibility to another staff member. I initially trained all my employees myself, but then I hired a consultant, who did a much better job. Eventually I promoted an existing member of staff to help with training and development. This was partly a financial decision, but it was also a control issue. Having my own training department meant I could roll out training as and when it was needed. This made a huge difference to my staff and the speed at which they learned.

Step 5 – set expectations

Before any training meeting, tell people what the training is about. This sets expectations and the standard to work to. If you take training and development seriously, expect your staff to, too. Continual communication helps with the way in which training is received.

This is also a great time to answer any questions that employees attending the training may have. Sometimes, people think they don't need to attend a particular course or refresher, so show them exactly why it is relevant to them. Perhaps they haven't performed in line with company objectives. Rather than having an embarrassing conversation in front of the other learners, address these concerns with individuals beforehand and make sure everyone is perfectly aligned with the training and development objectives.

Step 6 – track progress

If you use learning objectives for each procedure and keep updating your training matrix, you will find it straightforward to track individual progress towards company aims. You could also carry out regular one to ones to discuss employees' progress and find out what you can do to make their learning experience better. The ultimate goal of systems training is for staff to be able to follow the procedures and perform to company standards. If they're not performing, it's down to one of two things:

- **Lack of skill.** This is a training issue. With a well-thought-out and balanced training programme, this will happen less and less.

- **Lack of will.** This is a motivation issue. The person has chosen not to follow the procedures. In my experience, this is usually down to laziness or cutting corners. A robust training plan that ties in with an audit process will help prevent these issues. There's more on this in the 'Auditing' section of Chapter 3.

Step 7 – welcome feedback

With any training programme, you need effective feedback to see where you're doing well and where things could be improved. In my experience, many people don't appreciate constructive feedback and even shy away from it. Maybe it's a British thing, but people often get offended when others suggest improvements. But, as Bill Gates said:

> We all need people who will give us feedback.
> That's how we improve.

I once had an excellent business mentor who used to sit in on my managers' meetings. After every meeting, he would spend ten minutes with me explaining what I'd done well and what I needed to improve on. I really looked forward to these sessions, because this was the type of feedback I wouldn't get from my managers, who would be polite, clap at the right moments and laugh on cue at my terrible jokes. Flattering as it was, it wasn't going to help me grow as a businessman.

My mentor once picked me up on the fact that I swore in a managers' meeting – a major faux pas, and I didn't even notice I'd done it. It was hard to listen to this feedback, but it was important and I made sure it didn't happen again.

Feedback from learners – on individual sessions and group activities – is vital to improving the quality of your training and development programme, but if the overall trust isn't there, they will not be as forthcoming with their feedback. You need to create a culture that welcomes feedback, which is easier said than done.

You can do this by not overreacting or taking feedback personally. The first time you overreact to feedback you think is unfair, your staff will stop providing it. If you're the best trainer in the world and your learners are wrong, that isn't a problem – but that won't be the case.

If your employees are apprehensive about giving feedback, an anonymous survey could help. Feedback collected in this way will be less accurate and revealing than feedback given in a culture of openness and transparency, but it's still better than no feedback at all. You don't have to ask people lots of questions. I've seen feedback forms with as few as two questions: 'What did you like about the training session?' and 'What didn't you like about the training session?'

Once you've collated all the feedback, you need another dose of brutal honesty. Is the feedback relevant to the training? In other words, do your learners have a point? Be humble in the pursuit of continuous improvement – if they do have a point and you need to adapt or evolve your training, do it without stomping around like a bear with a sore head or taking it out on your staff. Make sure you thank people for their feedback and tell them you have improved the training. This will have a positive impact on learners and make your sessions better. Everyone wins.

Training paperwork

Documenting training isn't the most exciting part of the process, but it is one of the most important. Do you document your business plan, your finances, your procedures and your client contracts? Documenting training is just as important.

- It helps you to keep track of what training has been planned and received so you can review it regularly and be held accountable
- It ensures there is no ambiguity about what training has been agreed
- If you win the lottery tomorrow or get hit by a bus, someone else can take over
- If formal action is required as part of staff performance management, the training documents will be invaluable to your case

What should you document? Used alone, a skills training matrix and an individual learning plan (ILP) will benefit your businesses, training investment. Use both of them and you will have a really effective process that you can roll out to train almost any team in any industry.

Skills training matrix

A skills training matrix is a simple way of defining what skills are required for each role and where people are in relation to acquiring the skills to be successful in that role. It allows managers and team members to appraise how effectively they have demonstrated a skill over a set period, which may be a probation period or another agreed timeframe. It's a great tool to use with new starters and allows you to have a conversation about individuals' perceived effectiveness against what is needed in the role.

A job description is a great place to start, as this is the measure of what you want a person to bring to your business when you recruit them. You can always refer back to it at a later stage, too. You need to rate your staff on their ability to carry out certain actions in their job role.

I tried a few different rating systems before I found what works for my business. I have included the simple system I chose, but there are other good systems out there, so keep trying them until you find the one that's most appropriate for you and your business.

I would encourage you not to include a rating for 'average'. Forcing an appraisal to sit on one side or the other of average ensures that managers make decisions and don't just take the easy route. If you give managers the opportunity to rate an employee from one to five, most will choose the rating of three because they don't want to hurt the person's feelings by selecting a lower rating. The middle of the road doesn't attract attention. Anything less attracts negative attention: people want to understand why someone isn't performing better.

That's fine if you want a business where average performance slips under the radar. People might not be entirely comfortable with being forced to get off the fence, but this is the only way to know whether employees are performing well or whether they need more training or support.

The four performance criteria we use at Castledene are:

- **Underperforming.** The team member might not have had to use the particular skill that's being measured before. They may have demonstrated the skill at a higher level in the past, but shown a decline due to a change in a process, a system or their mind-set.
- **Developing.** The team member is developing the measured skill with coaching, training and practice, but they have not achieved the expected results yet.
- **Performing.** The team member is displaying the skill consistently and achieving the expected results, but there is room to develop further.

- **Exceeding.** The team member is displaying the skill at an exceptional level for their role and is able to coach and mentor others to develop their skills.

To record your skills matrix and appraisals, you can use anything from a printed form to a sophisticated software tool. This makes it easy to keep developing your skills-appraisal approach. I use the following simple Excel spreadsheet.

Skills Matrix - Portfolio Manager			
Name: John Smith			Branch: Hartlepool
Ref	Behaviours	Score	Performance Level
1	Positive attitude	3	Performing
2	Solution and results focused	3	Performing
3	Results orientated	2	Developing
4	Professionalism	4	Exceeding
5	Flexible approach	3	Performing
6	Committed to personal development	2	Developing
	Key competencies	**3**	
7	Ability to deliver excellent customer service as per charter	3	Performing
8	Developed time-management skills to ensure effective management of own resources	2	Developing
9	Ability to work under own initiative and as part of a team	3	Performing
10	Determination to secure new business with focused action	4	Exceeding
11	Negotiation skills to achieve the best outcome for the business and the customer	4	Exceeding
12	Conflict resolution within own levels of authority	3	Performing
13	Effectively manage staff	3	Performing
14	Enhanced communication skills	2	Developing

Behaviours. This refers to specific aspects of how you want your staff member to behave. You can rate each aspect of their behaviour accordingly. Always make sure you can back up the score with evidence and examples.

For example, at Castledene, once we have evidence that a member of staff has a positive attitude in all situations and they have been scored a four, we expect them to keep up that attitude at all times. But staff are not robots and we don't expect people to have a smile on their face 24/7, so we need to be pragmatic and warm in our approach to our staff.

Having said that, if someone scores a four, they shouldn't consistently go down to a three. They can't have undone the knowledge they demonstrated to hit a four. As difficult as it may be, the company must come first. If people are not showing the values or behaviours you expect, manage them out of the business.

Key competencies. These are the skills that you expect an employee to have to be able to do their job. Most people won't have all these skills from day one. As you train and develop them, their skills will grow and improve.

Again, a person shouldn't go backwards in their skill ratings. If they start to underperform, use the skills matrix to relate their performance back to their previous higher score. As brutal as this sounds, this evidence helps you if you need to performance manage someone out of the business.

Progression, not perfection, is the key. You can't expect people to be perfect from day one, but you can expect them to improve at an acceptable rate.

Key activities linked to KPIs. Linking tasks in people's job descriptions to certain KPIs means that you can measure their performance. The main advantage of KPIs is that people either achieve them or they don't, giving you factual evidence to help you manage people. As most KPIs are linked to the profitability of the company, you can also see the effect that individual employees have on the business at all times.

	Key activities (linked to KPIs)		
15	Chase arrears	3	Performing
16	Follow up viewings and feedback to landlords	2	Developing
17	Process appointments and feedback to landlord	1	Underperforming
18	Ensure that property maintenance issues are resolved in a timely & cost effective manner (including CP12s, etc)	2	Developing
19	Ensure MLITs are up to date for vacant properties	3	Performing
20	Answer all incoming communications (internal and external)	3	Performing
21	Deal with customer enquiries effectively (see customer service charter)	4	Exceeding
22	Ensure focus on own development	4	Exceeding
23	Resolve complaints	3	Performing
24	Escalate queries outside of own authority level	2	Developing
25	Maintain compliance with industry and internal regulations	3	Performing
26	Attention to all H&S issues, including hazard and accident reporting	2	Developing

If someone is achieving most of their KPIs, they may feel that they are a valuable asset to the company. While that may be true, if they're not hitting all their KPIs after receiving training, this suggests that they may not be the ideal person for the job. You only want the best staff for your business, whether they're the best from day one or you work to help them become the best. As a company, only keep people who want to better themselves.

Individual learning plan

An ILP helps you track employees' progress towards agreed goals and improvement activities. It should be updated after each review or development activity.

The key purpose of an ILP is to give each member of staff responsibility for their learning and for updating their ILP. Some managers shy away from this, usually because of the same old barrier to effective delegation: the belief that 'they won't do it as well as I do'. As a business leader or owner, you need to delegate to achieve the purpose of the systemisation process.

Documenting your own ILP is manageable. Grow your business and find yourself documenting fifty or 100 ILPs and it will take over your life. You need to empower staff, especially managers, to complete their own ILPs.

Use the documenting process as a coaching opportunity. Tell your staff what to include in their ILP and what level of detail you expect. The main reason for passing ownership of their development to your teams is to give them a sense of control.

There are five steps to creating and documenting an ILP. You can use these as table headings when reviewing.

Identify development needs. Have an honest and open skills appraisal with the employee. Together, decide where they are now and where they need to get to if they're to become a valuable member of your team based on your company's skills matrix. Once the person has been working with you for a short while, you will instinctively know what needs to be developed.

Consider development activities. Think about how you can help the employee to develop in the areas you have identified together. Will you do that yourself or get someone in who has more experience? You might have to train someone else to do this so you can take a step back. Identifying a leader in your business helps with this.

Set specific, measureable, achievable, realistic and time-bound (SMART) goals for development activities. Pay particular attention to the time-bound aspect, as this is likely to have a direct impact on how efficiently the results are delivered.

Review and evaluate the ILP. I cannot stress this enough. If you don't evaluate the outcome of the development activity from the last session, training is a waste of time and energy. Use your skills matrix to record improvements or use direct observations and feedback to build your team's confidence that they are heading in the right direction. Knowing how and in which areas your employees are developing is vitally important to your business.

Don't overcomplicate training and development. Start with the small things and work your way up, adding to your training and development programmes and ILPs over a number of years. The main thing is to make sure that they work for you and your staff. It's all well and good having the best operations manual in the world, but without the training and development to embed the information in your employees' minds, then it is a waste of time.

Staff are the lifeblood of your business so make sure they have every chance of succeeding.

TASK LIST – TRAINING AND DEVELOPMENT

- Design a skills matrix for every role in your business
- Make sure you are happy with all the behaviours, competencies and key activities
- Roll it out and ask the staff to score themselves
- Go away and get evidence as to why you agree or disagree with their scores

- In the next meeting (a month later), go over how you would score each staff member and why
- Design their training based on their development areas
- Relate back to the skills matrix if employees do not carry out actions or do work to a set standard
- Update every two or three months as the staff get better

FIVE

MANAGING STAFF

Managing staff is without doubt the hardest part of running any business. Why is that? Why does it have to be so hard? It should be easy, it should be predictable, so why are companies constantly having issues with staff management?

It is because many business owners and leaders don't understand how to manage and motivate staff – they think it's up to the staff to find their way of working and be motivated, even expecting them to manage themselves. But they are failing their staff if they have that attitude.

As business leaders, we need to give the employee the best chance of succeeding. If they don't after we have done everything in our power to help them, only then can we analyse things and see if it was our fault.

What do people crave? In a nutshell, we crave routine and goals. We need those two things in our lives, they're what make us get up in the morning and go to work without a feeling of dread.

Everyone loves a routine

Doing the same thing, day in, day out, sounds awful when you're a kid, so why do many of us love routine as adults? There are people out there who feel that without a schedule of work and activities, their lives would be lost.

It's because there are several wonderful benefits to having a routine.

Routines give comfort

What makes us comfortable? It's having the essential elements of life covered, allowing us to relax. Imagine what it's like to have no home, no food on the table, or a highly changeable partner or child. Having a massive degree of security, where we know what will happen next, is the key to comfort.

Routines are predictable

If you do a task 100 times and get the same result 100 times, it allows you to predict the future outcome. When you understand how things work, and more importantly, how you can influence a result, it allows you to relax. When situations arise from leftfield, they can catch you off guard, meaning that you have to put more energy into being aware.

Routines are safe

Some people say routines are like a comfort rut or personal cage. But look at it another way. If you take a zoo-raised lion out of its enclosure and put it in the wild, how do you think it will feel?

Routines, even those that are not good for us, often feel like places of sanctuary and safety because we know what to expect.

Routines make life simple

Simple equals easy to understand. When you know what your day will look like in a month or even a year's time, there are no unwelcome surprises in the pipeline. When you let go of stress, worry and anxiety, your mind can be clearer. Relaxation in many ways is the key to having good ideas, creativity and positivity in your life.

Routines allow space to learn

How much brain power do you have in a day? Do you find your energy and creativity run out the later it gets? If you have to donate your mental energy to worrying about what's coming next in life, this can sap your strength for imagination and positivity. What's more, if you are focusing constantly on the negatives of an unpredictable lifestyle, it can impact on the quality of your output.

Routines allow more productivity

Motivation will only get you so far in life. Look at New Year's resolutions as a prime example. To really get stuff done, as all the entrepreneurs say, you need discipline. What's the bedrock that forms the foundation of a good disciplined approach? Yes, routine. When you focus and double down on a task, it can be completed more quickly when you know how long it should take.

Routines make you feel relaxed and remove you from the punishing gaze of stress, which can become a string of personal put downs. With a good routine, you can cut down on the background noise, get more done, and form a habit that gets you out of bed and oiling the grindstone at 6am, even when it's dark, cold and tiring.

If you can't establish a good routine, what's really going on? Usually it's down to a lack of planning, methodology or simply unrealistic expectations. And while the young will always complain that routine is boring, the truth is that certain aspects of life are less than exciting. Having schedules and systems in place to run your business is the key to spending as little time as possible on the less than interesting things and giving yourself an easy life of management. Naturally, there have been cases where a business has been too inflexible to adapt and hence has missed out on opportunities, but such cases are hard to find.

Getting – and staying – motivated

I am a massive fan of motivational theories, so I think it is vital to explore how these methods and ideas can help turn your management practices from a struggle into a success.

Where should we start? For me, it has to be by looking at the needs that make us all human. Having these base desires met at some level is the spark behind every burning fire of activity and motivation.

Maslow's Hierarchy of Needs

You have probably heard of Maslow's Hierarchy of Needs, especially if you have been anywhere near a popular psychology book or self-help guide in the last thirty years. It's a well-known model of motivation, created by Abraham Maslow in the 1940s.

As with all theories, opponents can argue that the hierarchy is over simplified, but the five basic categories cover most of human experience, starting with essential physiological needs, moving upwards through safety and social needs towards the higher aims and objectives of human life, esteem and self-actualisation.

In Maslow's theory, the most powerful desire in any human being is to have their lowest unfulfilled need satisfied. As each level in life is adequately satisfied, they are motivated to move up to the next level. For instance, if someone is starving hungry, they don't care about having a place to sleep, but once that lowest need has been satisfied, it ceases to be a motivator. This is why people who have great houses, good diets and wonderful cars and businesses can pine for a lover or partner to share their success. Equally, as life experiences such as divorce or failure of business undermine higher needs, they can cause people to fall back down the hierarchy.

Maslow's Hierarchy of Needs is usually drawn as a pyramid. You'll find the basic desires in the bottom section and the higher aspirations at the top. Believe it or not, Maslow never actually put his ideas into this kind of diagram, but over the years the hierarchy and this image have become synonymous.

'What human beings can be, they must be,' Maslow famously said in 1954. Self-actualisation is therefore the highest section on the pyramid, representing an individual's desire to be all that they can be.

People love to use creative opportunities, tasks and outputs to define themselves against the myriad coloured canvases of the world. The top level of Maslow's hierarchy, self-actualisation, requires individuals to rally against their other needs, not simply achieve satisfaction at other levels. In plain English, this is about the sacrifices artists, scientists and global entrepreneurs have to make in order to get their personal success.

Alderfer's ERG Theory

What kind of needs do you need? Although Maslow gets all the headlines, he's not the only one with something to say about human desires. Clayton P Alderfer identified three steps or classes of needs:

- **Existence needs** – these are the individual's physiological and physical safety needs. You'll find Maslow's lowest needs in this tranche, which is defined by the basic human necessities. Think about non-negotiable aspects of life like shelter and food.

- **Relatedness needs** – everybody needs somebody, as the pop songs say. And this is what defines Alderfer's relatedness needs. Whether it's family relationships, friendships, working partnerships with peers, or intimate bonds with our partners, we need love, grounding and reciprocation. These are equivalent to Maslow's social and esteem needs.

- **Growth needs** – now we're talking about self-development, personal growth and finding the higher purpose of fitting into life. This final class is all about Maslow's self-actualisation needs.

McClelland's Human Motivational Theory

As with all science, theory forms a basis on which others build. One of the first to construct more thinking and ideas on top of Maslow's work was David McClelland. He believed that we acquire our motivators over time and there are three central drivers, one of which is always dominant in our personalities.

How do we go about determining the dominant motivator? It's dependent on all kinds of cultural experiences, life choices and our relationships – but it will always be one of:

- Achievement – a desire to succeed, to show others our mastery and ability

- Affiliation – the need to be loved, wanted and recognised as part of a group

- Power – control over our life, work and even the work of other people

You'll probably notice that McClelland is all about developing needs, while Alderfer and Maslow concentrate their ideas on satisfying needs that already exist within individuals.

Achievement motivation

As we've seen, this is the desire for not only success, but the chance to demonstrate mastery and supreme understanding of our chosen discipline. Naturally there are rewards associated with such mastery, such as high standards and personal material gain.

Individuals will often chase achievement and get satisfaction through praise from others, reaching personal goals and gaining success via singular activity and effort. For such people, luck does not even enter into the picture, but there are factors that can influence them in these directions, such as positive feelings and parents granting independence in childhood.

Motivation – the John Paul angle

We can always find another scientist, theorist or thinker to tell us about motivation, discipline and human needs, but for me, these three experts cover most of the ground. They demonstrate the importance of goal setting and ensuring that we have the basics nailed down when it comes to reaching for the stars.

Aiming for something bigger than ourselves, something challenging that's out there on the horizon, is bread and butter for the entrepreneur and business owner, but how does it relate to the way in which we can better manage our staff to get the best out of them? We can talk all we want about discovering values and looking for drivers, but individuals are rarely, if ever, that simple.

There will always be spanners in the works, especially when you think you have management and people nailed on. Don't stress at these times; remember that you've chosen a path of achievement and that's because you like flexibility and evolving challenges. So simply do what all great managers do. Roll up your sleeves and roll with the punches.

How to give managers a fighting chance

With the previous section in mind, we need to put a few things in place in the business to ensure we, as leaders, have a chance of being great and building the staff up to be as good as they can be. It always amazes me when managers are expected to perform miracles and turn around companies and teams in months, if not weeks, with no help from senior management or the business at large. It's a bit like pushing a boxer into the ring but tying his hands behind his back and telling him to hop on one leg – he has no chance of winning.

Procedures

We covered procedures in detail in Chapter 1, but they are worth mentioning here as they're the ultimate helping hand from a manager's perspective. They effectively set the rules and expectations for the business. Staff are expected to do XYZ in 123 timeframes. This makes it easy for managers to manage as the employee either carries out the action or they don't.

In organisations that don't have in-depth and well-documented processes, I often hear, 'I wasn't told to do that' or 'I didn't know that was my job' or even 'I didn't know it had to be to that standard'. This is a management nightmare. You can't successfully manage staff when there is no clarity and structure – see the theme here?

It's all about clear structure and format.

Imagine having an employee not doing what they should. You sit down to have a difficult conversation with them, and they say they didn't know they had to carry out a certain task in a certain way by a certain date.

You say, 'Yes you did, we had a chat about it last month.'

If you have no structured procedures in place, they can easily say – and it happens a lot, 'No we didn't, that was about something else' or 'I can't remember that conversation'. As frustrating as that is, there's little you can do. You know they do remember the conversation, but in the absence of structure and procedures, it's difficult to prove.

What this means is that the employee will at some point try it again. If they don't, then one of their colleagues will. This kind of response will spread, intentionally or otherwise. It needs to be nipped in the bud.

You do that by documenting every process in as much detail as possible. Now imagine the same conversation six months later.

Employee: 'I didn't know I had to do that.'

You: 'Yes, you did, as this is the procedure, you've signed the training document, and you have been doing the same process correctly for the last three months since we implemented the procedures.'

Employee: 'Erm...'

See the difference? It's hard for an employee to worm their way out of their responsibilities if it's all documented and everyone has clarity.

ILPs/skills matrix

We covered these in detail in Chapter 4, but why are they so important? Again, just like the procedures, they set expectations from a management perspective. They allow managers to know each employee's current training so when they are expected to carry out certain actions, they can't then turn around and say, 'I don't have the training.' You are cutting off the excuses list at the knees.

Some of you may not have heard that excuse yet, but you will. It happens to everyone at some point, and the bigger your business gets and the more staff you employ, the more often you will hear it.

From a motivational point of view, your IPLs and skills matrix documents are invaluable. They show the progression of the employees, where they were last year and where they are now, and also what the plan is for the rest of the year in terms of their development. They get and keep employees engaged. Remember the motivational theories – ambition, self-actualisation, esteem, etc? This is exactly what motivates people: seeing how they are moving forward towards goals.

Monthly one to ones

I'll go into more depth in this section as we haven't discussed one to ones as much as we have the previous topics.

It's likely many of you will have been on the wrong end of a poor one to one, so maybe you don't see the value in them. It's a real shame if that's the case as one to ones are an amazing tool to motivate and manage your staff to perform to the best of their ability.

To make a success of your monthly one to ones, you need to do them on a monthly basis. The clue is in the name. But they are not exactly the favourite option for many business owners and managers, which is mostly down to three reasons:

- Time – people don't prioritise them, so they are seen as a nuisance and put at the bottom of the to-do pile.
- No value – due to previous poor experiences.
- Confrontation – a lot of people think that one to ones are all about arguing and confrontation. It's not the case.

If you prioritise one to ones and do them consistently, they are an amazing tool to help improve the performance of the staff. They also don't take that long to do, especially if you are prepared. Once you become proficient, you could get them down to less than thirty minutes' preparation per one to one. They will also take less than an hour to carry out.

Some you will breeze through, while others, no matter how hard you try to pull out a conversation from the staff, you will get little back. This is fine, if they are performing. Some employees won't be able to stop talking, spouting irrelevant and nonsensical information at you. This is where experience pays dividends. The more one to ones you hold, the more adept you will be at pulling the employee back to the topic at hand and effectively chairing the meeting.

After the one to one, you can either ask a member of admin to write it up or outsource the write up, like we do at Castledene. If you insist on doing it yourself, allow another thirty minutes for the write up, but I don't recommend this as it's not a great use of your time. Providing you have made legible and good notes, outsourcing it is the better option.

I would say that once you become proficient, each one to one from start to finish will take, on average, one hour thirty minutes of your time. If you employ four staff, which is on average the amount an agency employs, then it's less than a day per month you need. The benefits will far outweigh the time you'll take.

I guarantee that once you implement monthly one to ones, things will come out of the woodwork from your staff that you didn't even know about, and then you can act. Staff, despite what they might tell you, like a formal environment to discuss certain topics. It makes them feel safe. Why do you think police interrogations are so formal? Police officers are trained to extract information, and you need to do the same.

The first time you hold a one to one with a staff member will be the most difficult as they may not have a base-line performance to discuss. However, you can relate their performance to the skills matrix. Don't worry if you haven't rolled one out yet, there's still time to do so. You see how everything fits in together? By having a skills matrix, you can talk about the employee's performance and base it on the skill level that they already have.

For example:

You: 'I want to chat about your arrears level, they seem to have increased.'

Employee: 'Have they? I haven't had the training, that's why.'

You: 'You have had training and have in the past had reduced arrears, showing that you know exactly what to do. It's not a training issue. Therefore, why have your arrears increased?'

It's a completely different conversation once you exclude training as an issue. It's now a motivational issue. You have it in black and white that the employee has chosen not to chase their arrears.

Playing devil's advocate, what if the employee said they didn't have time to chase the arrears?

You: 'You have had time management training so you are fully aware how to manage and prioritise your time. You have had the arrears training so you are aware of the impact of having high arrears. This is a motivational issue and you just haven't chased the arrears, is that correct?'

You have backed the employee into a corner. They have nowhere to go. Although it is a difficult situation for them – and it won't exactly be a bed of roses for you – they now know they will be pulled up if they don't carry out an expected action.

If you have these types of conversations a couple of times, staff will go one of three ways:

- They will get on board – they will realise accountability is here to stay
- They will fight against it – but from your perspective as everything is evidence based, it's easy to performance manage
- They will admit defeat by handing in their notice as they realise it's the only way to stop the conversations surrounding their non-performance

At Castledene, we have always found that when we manage effectively, we don't have to sack anyone. If they're not performing, they put their notice in. That's a sign of a good and well-managed business. There is nowhere for slackers to hide. All mistakes are highlighted, and employees know you will pull them up on it if they don't perform.

At the other end of the scale, should you praise your employees in a one to one? Absolutely, if they deserve it. This isn't an arse-kicking contest to see how many times you can say negative things to them. It's the perfect opportunity to build them up and let them know what they are doing well, so they can keep doing it. Praise where praise is due, and use evidence in the same way you would when you need to point out their failings. It will highlight that the one to one is fact and evidence based and subliminally state that there is no emotion involved. Your assessment is based on actual performance and is fair.

After each one to one, make sure you write it up in as much detail as possible. This needs to include parts of the conversation where the employee disagreed with you and their reasons for disagreeing. The write up needs to be an accurate and reflective account of the entire conversation as it may be needed if you ever have to terminate someone's employment, so make sure it's 100% correct.

Set the standard and get the written one to one back to the employee within forty-eight hours. It shows how important one to ones are, and the conversation will still be fresh in your mind so it will be a more accurate account. Ask the employee to read through it, and if they agree with it to send it back to you within twenty-four hours. If they don't, ask them to highlight what parts they disagree with and why. You then make a decision to change or keep the detail. Either way you want the one to one agreed and signed no later than five days after being carried out. Again, it's all about setting expectations for your staff.

Performance management

This is where the employee just isn't performing as they should be and you need to put them on extra measures. It's a bit like if your son or daughter needs extra maths or science tuition at school – nothing for that employee to be embarrassed about. It's meant to help them get better at their job, and in turn make the company better.

Employees will need to be put on performance management (PM) if they continually make the same mistakes or they duck out of carrying out certain actions, which is more common than you may think. PM is an in-depth and intense way of supporting your staff. You spend more time with them, either training and developing them or auditing their work to ensure they are doing it correctly. You will also be supporting them more frequently in various ways.

What does PM look like? You will plan out a PM process for however long you feel is necessary. For us, it's always three months. You then map out any additional training the employee may need to ensure they have the tools to perform the role to the required standard. After that, you may need to review their work on a weekly basis, so plan in those mini audits. The results need to be monitored, measured and managed as with all the other staff. That could be coupled with a feedback session to give the employee constructive feedback as to the standard and quality of their work.

You will need to support the employee more as this management is of the nurturing type that will either make or break the staff member. PM does take a lot of time, but in the main it is a huge benefit to staff and the business.

Of course, it doesn't always work, and that's fine. Sometimes it's best for both parties if people move to other businesses; that's just a part of life.

There are three things that you need to be aware of when you have to performance manage an employee:

Plan:

- Identify and clarify expectations
- Identify how results will be measured
- Agree the process with the employee
- Document the plan and expectations

Monitor:

- Evaluate the employee's progress
- Take action and support if necessary

Feedback:

- Review on an agreed basis (weekly and monthly)
- Sign off, renew PM cycle or terminate employment

There's not a lot more that you can do after PM. You have given the employee every chance of succeeding. It's all down to them now.

Communication

The secret to good management is clarity of communication. When you communicate, you set expectations, which are helped by things such as procedures and one to ones. But not everything will be documented or can wait until the one to one. Most management will be an ad hoc chat or meeting where something needs to be actioned.

You need to be clear on what you say and any actions that you need carrying out. For example:

You: 'I need you to contact the tenant at 1 Bourne Street by 1pm, please, to collect the arrears.'

I appreciate it may sound basic, but you may be amazed at how many times things won't get done to the standard you want them doing unless you literally spell out what you expect of the employee. You also need to be clear on any actions they may need to take to ensure the task gets done as you want it to.

You: 'I need you to contact the tenant at 1 Bourne Street by 1pm, please, to collect the arrears, and you need to collect at least £300 or we are serving notice.'

Imagine this scenario:

You: 'Did you contact 1 Bourne Street about the arrears?'

Employee: 'Yes, they said they can't pay.'

You: 'Oh, great, so what did you say?'

Employee: 'Nothing, they said they couldn't pay, so what do you expect me to do?'

You: 'AHHHHHHHH...'

See the point? If the employee continually shows zero initiative or their attitude is poor, then you can performance manage them easily. Attitude and initiative are abilities and can therefore be measured and managed.

Fairness

It stands to reason that being fair is a great management trait, but things happen in business that make staff think there are favourites in the workplace. Do not under any circumstance let this happen.

Anyone who has followed me or read my stuff realises how great I think my MD Adele is in her approach to management. She, over the years, formed a good friendship with one of the people we employ. They met up outside of work and socialised on a weekend. But in work, Adele managed her exactly the same as she managed anyone else. The staff member didn't expect any special treatment or benefits, which was a good thing as she would have been disappointed. Adele has the highest of standards and wouldn't have changed her management any way.

I'm sure that some of the staff passed gossip among themselves about how this staff member got special treatment, but there was absolutely zero evidence to support this. Had it been brought up as an issue, then it could easily have been addressed.

Staff have long memories and tend to bring things up from years back – 'Oh, but it was OK for Sophie to finish early that time back in 2013' – even though it may not be relevant to the current conversation. This is why family-run businesses are hard to manage as most owners tend to favour their children or other family members, giving them roles in the business that they are not suitable for.

John Maxwell, who is an international best-selling leadership author and public speaker, developed the five levels of leadership, the bottom level being position. In other words, at this level people will follow the leader due to their title and nothing else. I have seen this on countless occasions in family-run businesses.

Just for the record, when my brother and I worked at my dad's factory, he made sure we started off at the bottom and had zero influence over the staff. This was completely the right call to make, ensuring the guys on the shop floor accepted us. By starting at the bottom, we earned their respect.

I will cover the five levels of leadership in more detail in Chapter 8.

Reward and recognition

A major part of any good management structure is knowing when to praise and recognise employees' efforts and performance. There is a lot of empirical evidence to suggest that rewarding and recognising employees lifts the sprits and keeps motivation high. It's also common sense, to be blunt. No one likes to repeatedly get an arse kicking or be ignored, so rewarding staff or recognising their efforts where appropriate has a beneficial effect.

There are lots of theories, but my personal view is to reward staff when they hit their goals or go above and beyond what is expected of them. If their target is five lets and they achieve five, then I give them a pat on the back or tell them 'Well done'. That little 'Well done' takes no effort at all from me, but may mean the world to them. But I'm not a believer in giving out praise for missing targets. Maybe it is my sporting background or the no-filter way I view things, but I'm not into participation trophies or certificates for taking part. Not my thing.

My staff know and appreciate that if I say 'Well done' then I mean it, and it probably means more to them than throwaway praise that is bandied around all the time.

How do you recognise or reward your staff? This will vary from company to company. At Castledene, we have monthly awards where we recognise:

- Branch of the month (BoM)
- Employee of the month
- Prospector of the month

For the winner of BoM, my team and I take the staff out for a meal after work, and the other two more personal awards get an afternoon spa break. It doesn't cost a lot of money, but it means a lot to them.

There are other ways to reward staff: time off, shopping vouchers, etc. My team and I have found that rewarding the staff with something that creates a memory is much better than a short-term fix such as chocolate or wine that will be gone by the weekend. Spa breaks are talked about for weeks if not months after the event, motivating the other staff as they will hear the stories and want the exact same thing.

To summarise, you don't need hundreds of management theories, although I do enjoy reading and researching them. You just need to do the basics and do them well. Understand that staff crave routine and structure, and do everything you can to give them that so they become easier to manage.

TASK LIST - MANAGEMENT

- Write the procedures down so employees know the rules of the business
- Carry out one to ones – give structure and a formal setting to accountability
- Design and implement ILPs/skills matrix that identify current training standards and what is needed for employees to become better
- Carry out PM for those who need additional training and support
- Be fair – we all want to be treated fairly
- Have great communication – the best managers are always great communicators
- Don't forget about reward and recognition – let people know they are doing a good job

You get the fundamentals right and you will be a good manager. I am a believer that you can vastly improve your management skills in a short space of time if you put in the work and the effort.

SIX

KEY PERFORMANCE INDICATORS

Why are KPIs important?

From reviewing employee performance to tracking company progress, there are a number of reasons why KPIs are an important factor in assisting your company's growth.

Measure your targets

Though they may be easily confused, KPIs are not company goals or targets themselves; they're a *measurement* of goals and targets. For instance, if your company goal is to tenant or take on a certain number of properties, your KPIs will show you how close or far you are from reaching that goal. A KPI in this instance may indicate that your valuer is only converting 40% of the valuations he or she is being invited out to. As a manager in this situation, you are instantly made aware of your employee's progress and the reason they are not hitting the desired conversions.

When you're able to measure your goals this way, it gives you the opportunity to see where you're going wrong, and subsequently make decisions that help you reach your goals faster. This is arguably the most important reason why KPIs should be used as it's the most significant use of a KPI.

Continuous learning

Being able to measure targets using KPIs can create a learning atmosphere within your company. When you notice an unfavourable reading on a KPI – maybe lots of viewings but low conversions in lettings – you have the chance to talk to the individual or team involved with that specific KPI. This a great opportunity for you to teach the employees how to do things differently and perform better in order to reach set targets.

Additionally, you can analyse whether the set KPIs are an effective measurement, and make necessary modifications if the employee feels that the targets are unrealistic. It's all about communicating with the staff about their performance and receiving feedback.

Receive important information

KPIs provide an immediate snapshot of the overall performance of your company. When you're in a highly competitive market, that information can be a crucial part of your attempts to beat your competition. Are you selling more houses than them? What's your conversion rate like in comparison? The real-time data that KPIs provide allows you to make systematic adjustments so that you're not left making frantic changes at the end of each month to reach your goals.

Encourage accountability

Without KPIs revealing vital statistics about performance, you run the risk of making inaccurate decisions about employees during reviews. You may assume that an employee is performing poorly because he/she has punctuality issues or a perceived lack of company engagement, but you have no quantifiable proof. A KPI may reveal that your assessment is incorrect and the perceived 'poor performer' has some favourable stats and delivers good results. On the other hand, poorly performing employees can hardly argue their case if their KPI stats show unfavourable readings.

Essentially, KPIs encourage accountability for both employees (if they're not performing) and employers (if KPIs are deemed unreachable). In any PM situation, you need to have proof to back up your statements and KPIs are the best way to do that. No more 'I feel you have not been performing' or 'I think you have had a poor month'. It's a case of yes or no, black or white.

Boost morale

Employee motivation and job satisfaction are extremely important to improve company performance and culture. It can often be difficult to motivate your team when set targets can only be achieved once a quarter or once a year, so allow employees to receive positive reports for meeting certain KPIs in the short term. The results are often instant, which creates a sense of purpose and keeps them focused on meeting their goals.

A good KPI system will increase the number of goals met by keeping your managers abreast of their team's performance. They could use this information to document employees' actions and progress, discuss their findings, provide feedback, and ultimately increase job satisfaction as forthcoming targets are met.

Which KPIs should you have?

This is the most common question I get asked when I speak about KPIs. I always do the same thing: I turn it around and ask a question myself:

'What do you think you need to know to improve the business and why?'

It gets the person thinking. They generally come back with the usual suspects: numbers of lets, sales, valuations to listing, listing to sales, etc, and they are all good answers. I then follow it up with:

'If you had any of this information, could you use it to manage your staff better and get more from them?'

If they say yes, then they already know the correct KPIs to implement. You see, having the wrong KPIs is just as bad as having no KPIs. It means you are concentrating on the wrong information and you can't make the correct decisions. It wastes time and forces you to lose focus.

Who should have KPIs?

Every person in your business should have at least two KPIs, be they operational or financial. If you can't find out how and in what way to measure someone's performance, then you have to ask yourself a question: 'Are they useful to my business?'

Even contractors can have KPIs:

- Quality of work – you could check it and rate it
- Speed of response at various stages of the job
- Feedback from tenant, ie satisfaction survey
- Speed of invoicing
- Complaints received about them
- Length of time taken to carry out a regular job

Everyone needs KPIs – only surround yourself with good-quality people whose performance you can measure.

Once you have KPIs in your business, the only question is how to manage people when they don't produce the results, which will be in black and white in front of you. Before they could have talked their way out of it. You didn't know, they didn't know, no one knew how they were really performing, but that all changes with KPIs. You know categorically if they are performing in line with the individual and company goals and targets.

Some of the KPIs we have at Castledene are pretty basic and some are slightly more complex, but they all have to affect the bottom line at some point. There's no point using them otherwise. Why measure something that doesn't make you money?

Even customer satisfaction and other less tangible metrics relate back to the bottom line. If your customer service is high, then you will have a decent bottom line, unless you really can't operate a business.

For our portfolio managers, my team and I monitor the key metrics such as:

- Income generated from commission they've collected
- Income generated from tenant-find fees
- Income generated from inventories, renewals, etc
- Income generated from repairs

It's all money in the bank, not invoiced. It has to be cleared funds as that's what pays the bills.

You can target people on other measurements in the business, but I'll give you a little idea about how this can backfire. We don't monitor:

- Viewings – employees can easily organise low quality and unfiltered viewings
- Properties tenanted – employees can discount fees just to get people in, giving a false positive
- Properties brought on – an employee could bring in lots of poor-quality properties

The three KPIs above are common in a lot of agencies, but they can be manipulated and bent to benefit the individual at the expense of the organisation, which is why we don't use them. It's worth noting that a metric we do use is average income per property. This way we know what another twenty properties should be worth to us as a company.

Don't try and overcomplicate things in this business – keep it simple.

Branch managers

Our branch managers (BMs) are heavily driven on the financials of the business. We share the profit and loss figures with them all. Can I hear some of you gasping right now? But why not?

What happens if you hire someone to drive the business forward, expect them to boost income and generate profit, but don't share the figures with them? That to me is poor business acumen and says you don't trust your staff. Share everything with them. What's the worst that can happen – they tell people? So what? Do you really care?

Let's flip the coin and look at what can happen if you do share the figures with them. You get buy in, they feel engaged, they feel trusted, they work harder for you and get better results. When you look at it like that, the positives far outweigh the negatives.

For our BMs at Castledene, it's all about the profit and loss. Why wouldn't it be? Every action they take must be aligned with the goal of hitting their branch targets, which are financial and impact on the profit and loss. If they take on X amount of properties, then we know it will produce Y income. If they rent out X properties at a minimum of Y per let, then it will produce Z income. If they get X renewals, inspections, etc, it will produce Y income. If they lack in one area, say new properties, then they need to make up for it in other areas. Instead of doing twelve lets, for example, they need to do fourteen, and so on. We make them accountable for their performance and their staff's performance. That way, the BMs won't hide or look after any non-performing staff as it brings the whole branch down.

What KPIS not to have

People either have no KPIs at all or have far too many – it's a common paradox. Do you really care how many toilet rolls one of your branches uses or the miles one of the company cars has done or viewings on a Monday after 4pm? Will knowing this information make you money? Is measuring it the best use of your or your staff's time?

Having too many KPIs means the essential things won't get consistently measured, and if they're not consistently measured then they won't be managed and will fall by the wayside. Don't measure things that no one cares about. Don't measure things that might be a whim and you won't follow up on. Don't measure things that no one is totally accountable for, there is no point. It's a waste of your time.

How to present your KPIs

There is lots of software out there that can do this: Qlik, Target Dashboard, SimpleKPI, BOARD, Scoro, Datapine, Bilbeo, to name a few. They all have their pros and cons so I won't get into them all, as it's up to you to see which one:

- Fits your budget – they massively vary in price
- Fits your strategy
- Can pull the information from your various software

The main issue is that some of them won't talk to Xero or SAGE or whatever property customer-relationship management (CRM) system you are using.

At Castledene, we are in the process of building our own software with a developer and are hoping to have that up and running in a few months. It will be a one-stop shop for all the KPIs and produce some elegant dashboards in real time, accessible to us anytime from anywhere.

The great thing about having dashboards is that you can get all the information you want from anywhere in the world at any time, which sets the standard for others to live up to in your business. There is no hiding.

Data is what runs businesses, and the way you look after that data is the difference between success and failure. Not just from a compliance perspective, but also from a profitability perspective. You don't have to spend fortunes on fancy specialist dashboard software – when Castledene first started, I used a simple Excel spreadsheet that I populated manually. It was quite time consuming, so I hired an expert for a few days to build a dashboard, but it still had to be populated manually. It did the job, though.

I then wanted an all singing and dancing dashboard that integrated with the company's software systems and gave complete transparency not only for my leadership team, but also in the branches.

TASK LIST - KPIS

- Have a look in your business and see what information you deem to be important to manage your company
- If you had that information, could you use it to improve performance?
- Pick the KPIs you want to measure in your business
- Understand what information you need to measure the KPIs
- Start managing your business using KPIs – test and tweak
- Share results with your staff

SEVEN

FINANCIAL MANAGEMENT

If you're not keeping score, you're just practising.
Vince Lombardi

This is probably my favourite quote of all time. The score Vince Lombardi is referring to is the ability to measure your performance. In business terms, that score is financial and operational.

You measure the performance of your business by keeping track or score on a daily, weekly, monthly and annual basis. This chapter will show you why and how you do this in your business.

It is of critical importance that you take the numbers in your business seriously. In fact, I would go as far as saying that if you don't, you shouldn't be in business. You try getting a loan or investor if you don't know your business numbers or performance. You can't, it's impossible. So, if investors, banks, funders, etc see it as important, you must too.

We will talk about the financial documents – profit and loss, the balance sheet and cash flow – in this chapter. All of these are integral to your business, so I recommend you fine tune or implement them straight after you have read this handbook.

Profit and loss

The profit and loss (P&L) statement is one of the three financial statements that are imperative in the running of your business. It gives you a snapshot over a period of time of what you have invoiced for and what you have been invoiced for. It assumes that there is no bad debt and all invoices will be paid. It does *not* give you a cash-flow position, as some people think, the main reason being that most invoices are not paid on the day they are received, and some will have payment terms, eg thirty or sixty days. P&L is also known as management accounts, and banks and investors insist on seeing your P&L documents if they are looking at investing in or loaning money or assets to your business.

I cannot stress enough the importance of P&L and how much it has changed my business for the better. I know to the penny how my branches are performing and if they are hitting their financial targets. In the previous chapter on KPIs, all the targets are related to financials. Well, this is the part of the financials that they relate to.

Imagine knowing exactly and precisely what sort of a month you've had – being able to target each staff member on performance, know whether they hit their targets and the company benefited financially, and tell to the penny how that affected the organisation. It still astounds me that some businesses don't have monthly management accounts. This is mainly because the business leader is:

- Lazy – simple as that. The business leader can't be bothered. If that's the case with you, to be blunt, you will never be a success in business.
- Scared of the information they will show. I get it. It's a bit like looking at your bank account when you are low on funds. I was there when I first started in business. But you need to 'pull up your big boy/girl pants' and get on with it.
- Not sure where to start. This is the most common reason I hear for businesses not having P&L, and it's the easiest to answer. As a business leader, it's not your job. That's what a bookkeeper or accountant is for.
- Worried it's too expensive. Load of rubbish – you can get a bookkeeper for a small agency for around £200 per month, if not less. If this is too much for you, then you need to budget in order to get a bookkeeper in your business. Once you have the financial information, you can target the staff to perform. I guarantee – and I don't do that very often – your staff will perform better.
- Not making P&L a priority. Honest, but a load of bullshit. If you don't prioritise financial management highly enough to have management accounts, then you really need help in prioritising.

Joe Bloggs Lettings Ltd

Profit and Loss 2017 – 2018

	April	May	June	July	Aug
Branch Income					
Management Commission	7845.00	7654.00	8904.33	7641.23	8845.55
Tenant Find Fees	1628.33	2692.80	2575.00	4189.20	3176.00
Admin Fees	1108.33	1094.00	1600.00	900.00	780.00
Inventories and Mid Terms	90.00	0.00	0.00	90.00	90.00
Tenancy Renewals	237.00	230.00	734.00	310.00	490.00
Repairs	242.50	366.17	282.17	730.00	0.00
Misc	300.00	1540.00	-111.71	202.50	718.80
Sales	0.00	1250.00	0.00	1250.00	0.00
Interest Received	0.02	0.03	0.04	0.00	0.00
	11451.18	**14827.00**	**13983.83**	**15312.93**	**14100.35**

	April	May	June	July	Aug
Cost of Sales					
Motor Vehicle Lease	758.56	759.34	134.56	134.56	134.56
Motor Vehicle Fuel	30.00	157.02	45.00	0.00	0.00
Motor Vehicle Insurance	53.00	53.00	53.00	53.00	53.00
Misc. Motor Expenses	29.41	27.71	-63.69	111.83	24.31
Other Purchase Costs	133.18	350.86	926.26	665.70	480.64
	1004.15	**1347.93**	**1095.13**	**965.09**	**692.51**
Direct Expenses					
Marketing and PR	0	81.25	81.25	81.25	81.25
Property Portals	500.00	520.00	520.00	520.00	520.00
Advertising	182.00	114.99	75.99	0.00	0.00
	682.00	716.24	677.24	601.25	601.25
Gross Profit/(Loss)	**9765.03**	**12762.83**	**12211.46**	**13746.59**	**12806.59**

Sep	Oct	Nov	Dec	Jan	Feb	YTD
9032.44	8875.44	9104.55	9234.33	9077.44	9343.22	95557.53
2318.80	3115.79	1487.50	3156.00	834.00	4303.00	29476.42
700.00	1335.00	1305.00	795.00	1380.00	1740.00	12737.33
0.00	0.00	108.00	76.00	130.00	90.00	674.00
283.33	205.00	270.00	527.00	760.00	515.00	4561.33
0.00	0.00	0.00	220.00	283.60	253.70	2378.14
1046.67	1079.90	337.66	828.80	80.00	127.00	6149.62
0.00	4260.00	3300.00	3000.00	2400.00	0.00	15460.00
0.09	0.02	0.00	0.04	0.00	0.00	0.24
13381.33	**18871.15**	**15912.71**	**17837.17**	**14945.04**	**16371.92**	**166994.61**

Sep	Oct	Nov	Dec	Jan	Feb	YTD
134.56	134.56	134.56	134.56	134.56	134.56	2728.94
0.00	0.00	10.00	10.00	0.00	0.00	252.02
128.09	53.00	53.00	53.00	53.00	53.00	658.09
58.34	89.17	93.33	64.17	64.17	64.17	562.92
305.42	552.63	500.40	227.82	453.26	206.79	4802.96
626.41	**829.36**	**791.29**	**489.55**	**704.99**	**458.52**	**9004.93**

Sep	Oct	Nov	Dec	Jan	Feb	YTD
81.25	81.25	81.25	418.21	81.25	206.25	1274.46
675.00	500.00	500.00	500.00	500.00	500.00	5755.00
46.00	20.00	412.56	214.52	455.50	600.00	2121.56
802.25	601.25	993.81	1132.73	1036.75	1306.25	9151.02
11952.67	**17440.54**	**14127.61**	**16214.89**	**13203.30**	**14607.15**	**148838.66**

Overheads				
Gross Wages	4427.34	4868.30	4746.57	5016.76
Employer Costs	273.78	279.30	262.724	289.79
Rent	750.00	750.00	750.00	750.00
Rates	447.12	0.00	0.00	0.00
Light and Heat	221.91	0.00	0.00	0.00
Insurance	96.97	96.97	115.22	110.22
Cleaning	17.00	27.75	24.56	94.17
HR and H&S	9.80	9.80	9.80	9.80
Accountancy	345.83	345.83	345.83	345.83
Solicitors	8.00	8.00	8.00	8.00
Telephone Calls	34.06	26.22	0.00	0.00
Telephone Maintenance and Support	205.00	205.00	185.00	168.00
Stationery	0.00	24.19	252.43	93.04
Printing	304.49	0.00	0.00	129.00
Postage	115.50	36.28	49.81	62.31
Equipment Hire and Maintenance	152.00	152.00	151.99	99.29
Sundry Expenses	0.00	10.00	55.99	88.02
IT Software Lease	164.00	164.00	164.00	164.00
IT Support	87.50	87.50	0.00	93.23
Computer Licences	80.80	78.93	78.93	78.93
Subscriptions	16.25	16.25	16.25	16.25
Bank Interest & Charges	60.60	25.39	39.00	38.90
	7817.95	**7211.71**	**7256.12**	**7655.54**
Net Profit/(Loss)	**-2061.71**	**5551.12**	**4955.34**	**6091.05**

016.76	5093.68	5070.03	4694.82	4331.78	5115.17	5241.84	53623.05
289.79	270.49	307.46	337.81	261.65	316.84	261.64	3151.29
50.00	750.00	750.00	750.00	750.00	750.00	750.00	8250.00
0.00	0.00	0.00	60.00	0.00	0.00	0.00	507.12
20.00	112.68	203.00	190.51	304.90	369.66	362.98	1885.64
110.22	35.13	110.22	110.22	110.22	110.22	110.27	1115.88
253.75	0.00	24.00	76.92	17.00	30.00	21.00	586.15
9.80	9.80	9.80	9.80	9.80	9.80	9.80	107.80
45.83	345.83	345.83	345.83	345.83	345.83	358.83	3817.13
8.00	8.00	8.00	8.00	8.00	35.00	8.00	115.00
26.84	0.00	0.00	0.00	0.00	0.00	0.00	87.12
68.00	168.00	168.00	168.00	168.00	168.00	168.00	1939.00
0.00	-9.20	29.64	13.18	0.00	17.57	38.38	459.23
0.00	350.00	0.00	99.00	149.00	131.77	653.00	1816.26
53.22	0.00	24.04	154.72	92.00	20.00	120.00	727.88
178.22	99.29	231.06	99.29	99.29	99.29	99.29	1461.01
0.00	0.00	0.00	0.00	0.00	40.00	96.25	290.26
64.00	164.00	164.00	164.00	164.00	164.00	164.00	1804.00
447.62	274.00	172.14	109.13	76.33	172.69	167.68	1687.82
78.93	78.93	78.83	40.40	60.40	86.93	86.93	828.94
16.25	16.25	16.25	16.25	0.00	0.00	0.00	130.00
13.30	35.20	19.60	39.05	77.22	44.32	119.67	512.25
50.53	**7802.08**	**7731.90**	**7486.93**	**7025.42**	**8027.09**	**8837.56**	**84902.83**
56.06	**4150.59**	**9708.64**	**6640.68**	**9189.47**	**5176.21**	**5769.59**	**63935.83**

What should my P&L look like?

This is subjective and will vary from person to person, but it needs to contain all the information that you want to measure. At Castledene, it's all about the income as our costs are pretty stagnant, although I do measure them for anomalies. Whatever income I want to measure, I will note in the income part of the P&L.

As you can see from the above P&L illustration, all the various income streams, from management income to tenant-find fees and renewals and sales, are measured so the business can manage and target the staff. What's important is that it's done over an annual period so you can see any good or bad months and analyse why they happened. You can see if you have an upward or downward trend on performance and alter management and leadership to suit.

For example, the overall income may be high and steady due to excess commission or a flurry of renewals, but the tenant-find fees may be low. Unless you measure all aspects of your business income, you will never know. As the move-in process can take a few weeks, if not months, since most tenants have to give four weeks' notice, it can take a long time to turn around the performance *unless* it is noticed at an early stage. In other words, trouble trouble before it troubles you.

You will next have a cost-of-sales section on your P&L. What costs were needed to make your sales? If you ran a manufacturing company, it would be materials. In a service company, costs of sales are always low.

Some accountants/bookkeepers will have different ideas, believe it or not, as to what a cost of sale is. If I'm honest, I don't place a huge amount of importance on it, as it has little influence over my income and overheads, which to me are the most important things.

You then have overheads, which I find fascinating as they are crucial to your P&L. This is your time to see exactly what it costs to run your business. Can you improve the costs and reduce them?

I've yet to find a client or customer who can't save themselves money once they have implemented a robust financial management strategy. Without one, people can't see the wood for the trees, so they don't know what they are spending resources on. Especially with the tenant fee ban in England due, we need to be careful with all our expenditure in our industry.

The best figure one of my clients saved was over £36,000, which accounted for around 15% of the agency's income. We did this in fewer than twenty-four hours. The owner was spending far too much money on marketing, insurance and utilities, but they didn't know exactly what they were spending. Once it was staring them right in the face, they were shocked. They halved their Rightmove spend, cut back on a pointless branding exercise, and reduced their insurance and utilities spending by a considerable margin.

I can't stress enough how important it is to have a monthly P&L for the financial year to date. You must have the ability to compare and contrast at least on a quarterly basis. For example, if you look at IT support in the illustration, it jumps from around £90 per calendar month to £447.62. There may be a genuine reason for this, but at a glance you can see it and ask probing questions as to why there was a sudden jump. This helps you in budgeting for next year, which puts you in a better position to perform.

Share the P&L with your staff to show them where you are. You may not feel comfortable with this, but you will get more buy in and engagement if you trust them and are transparent with them.

Balance sheet

Most business owners can get their heads around the P&L, but the balance sheet can be a step too far. The P&L is a snapshot over a period of time, but the balance sheet is a snapshot of a particular minute. It states what assets the business owns and what it owes – its liabilities – on a particular date.

The balance sheet is used to show how the business is being funded and how the funds are being used. It is used in three ways:

- For reporting purposes (limited company's annual accounts)
- To help interested parties – such as investors, creditors or shareholders – assess the worth of your business at a given moment
- To help you analyse and improve the management of your business

A strong balance sheet, ie one showing low debt and high assets, adds real value to a company, while the opposite, high debt and low assets, could mean the company is not worth much. Savvy investors, banks, etc all look at the strength of a balance sheet. They can get this information, or an abbreviated version of it, from a company's main office.

I always look at my competitors' balance sheets, especially when they make claims about how well they are doing. You may not be surprised to know that I discover many aren't doing as well as they claim.

The assets side of the balance sheet includes cash, inventories (sometimes called stock) and property. It also includes some things that you can't touch, like any difference between the value of assets the business has purchased and the price it paid for them. This is called 'goodwill'.

The liabilities on the balance sheet include bank loans, any money owed to the company's creditors – often other companies that have supplied goods and services but not yet been paid – and money set aside to pay for things in the future, like pensions or tax bills. When you subtract the liabilities from the assets, anything that's left over belongs to the owners of the company and its shareholders. These shareholders' funds can also be expressed as the amount that shareholders initially put into the company plus any profits they've retained at the end of each year of trading.

What are assets?

Balance sheets usually distinguish between short-term assets, usually less than a year old and called 'current' by accountants, and longer-term assets, called 'fixed'. Fixed assets are things such as property, other businesses you might have bought, and anything that is 'fixed down'. Current assets are things that can easily be liquidated or converted into cash. In the illustration, cash in the bank and debtors, ie people who owe the company money, can, in theory, be recalled.

What are liabilities?

These are items that a business owes to other people, and they are also split between short and long term, or amounts falling due within one year and amounts falling due after one year. Amounts due within one year could be things like pay as you earn (PAYE) tax, suppliers' fees, VAT, Her Majesty's revenue and customs (HMRC), short-term loans, overdrafts. Amounts falling due after more than one year will be long-term loans.

Retained earnings

This is a good way of looking at the profitability of the company. I've known it to be called profit and loss or cash in bank, but it effectively means cash that the company has at its disposal if need be. This again gives a reasonable suggestion as to the profitability of the business.

Experienced people with financial capability understand the benefits of retained earnings. This doesn't mean you now have to go and sign up for an accounting degree, but having the ability to read a balance sheet, or any financial statement for that matter, is imperative for your financial education.

Cash flow

If a business runs out of cash and is not able to obtain new finance, it will become insolvent. It is no excuse for management to claim that they didn't see a cash-flow crisis coming.

In business, cash is king. Cash flow is the lifeblood of all businesses – particularly start-ups and small enterprises. As a result, it is essential that management forecast (predict) what is going to happen to cash flow to make sure the business has enough to survive.

Here are the key reasons why a cash-flow forecast is so important:

- It identifies potential shortfalls in the cash balances in advance. Think of the cash-flow forecast as an early warning system. This is, by far, the most important reason for a cash-flow forecast.
- It makes sure that the business can afford to pay its suppliers and employees. Suppliers who don't get paid will soon stop supplying the business. It is even worse if employees are not paid on time: they will walk out the door.

- It spots problems with customer payments. Preparing the forecast encourages the business owner to look at how quickly customers are paying their debts. Note – this is not really a problem for businesses like retailers that take most of their sales in cash/credit cards at the point of sale.
- It's an important discipline of financial planning. The cash-flow forecast is a management process, similar to preparing business budgets.

External stakeholders such as banks may require a regular forecast. Certainly, if the business has a bank loan, the bank will want to look at cash-flow forecasts at regular intervals. I've never borrowed from any organisation that hasn't wanted to see some sort of financial management statements.

You can have a monthly cash-flow forecast or a weekly one, just as long as you are planning how cash rich you are regularly. Depending on which statistics you look at, 25–45% of small businesses go out of business due to poor cash flow, not poor sales or staff. By having a cash-flow statement, you can see the potential issues before they become business threatening.

Help with your financial statements

What to look for in a bookkeeper/accountant

Let's assume you appreciate that financial statements are of the utmost importance in your business, but you don't know where to get the relevant people to do the job. It's simple: first speak to your accountants, who will either be able to do it for you or recommend bookkeepers that they work with. Using a bookkeeper or your accountant to prepare the books for the annual accounts or the quarterly value-added tax (VAT) will save you money on an annual basis. If all else fails, use good old Google for recommendations.

Ask to speak to a couple of clients of the bookkeeper, ideally in the same industry as you, to see if they have a happy customer base. Some bookkeepers will say it doesn't matter if they have worked in the same industry before as accounts are accounts, but that's not true. A bookkeeper with property experience will have an advantage.

You need to set the parameters:

- What's included in the cost?
- How quickly will you get your financial statement? You need it as quickly as possible in the new month (ideally in the first week).
- How will the financial statement be laid out?
- Where will certain expenses go on the balance sheet?
- Will you be able to liaise with your accountant as the financial statement will form part of the bigger tax strategy?

Xero/SAGE/QuickBooks/other

Most bookkeepers and accountants will have their favourite software, but that's irrelevant. You need information in a timely manner in a format that you are happy with, so don't make any allowances for them. They work to your parameters or not at all. It's your business and you live or die by your business decisions.

At Castledene, we use SAGE and Xero, depending on the size of the branch. SAGE tends to be better for larger businesses and Xero for smaller businesses with fewer transactions, but providing it can produce the information you want, it doesn't really matter what software you use.

TASK LIST – FINANCIAL MANAGEMENT

- Get your accountant or bookkeeper on board as soon as possible.
- Agree the format you want.
- Income needs to be split into various streams that you can measure and manage.
- Overheads – you need to agree what goes where. Don't rely on the bookkeeper to automatically know.
- Get your documents over a twelve-month period and year to date.
- Scrutinise every entry on a monthly basis.
- Share it with your staff – be brave and do it!

EIGHT

LEADERSHIP

As with Chapter 3, I'm not going to reinvent the wheel when it comes to my thoughts on leadership. I covered this in detail in my previous book *From Stress To Success*, so I've just added a few upgrades here.

I have an MD who runs my business and business partners who run my other ventures. This is by design. Yes, I had to put work in at the start to build the business up to the point where I could recruit a leader, but essentially, either I have to be a leader or someone else has to be.

You need a captain to sail a ship, a pilot to fly a plane, and a leader to drive the business forward. You can't build an empire of multiple businesses and run them yourself. You can have all the best systems in the world, an auditing process to be proud of and a feedback loop that would put Disney to shame, but without identifying a leader to take control of the organisation, you are still a slave to the business.

One of the main reasons for having a systemised company is that you don't have to work if you don't want to. But this only works if you have someone else to lead and take the company forward. Having a systemised business is all about choices, and having a leader gives you those choices. They handle all issues with staff, customers, HR, finances, etc. They're the true secret to scaling your business.

Why do people find it hard to hand over control of their business to someone else? It's a combination of things. Business owners can be precious about their businesses and I can understand that. I used to be like that. They look for exact replicas of themselves, they look for the finished article, they look for a better version of themselves, and that is a huge mistake. It's never going to happen.

There is only one of you, and thank goodness for that. Imagine two? I couldn't think of anything worse than two John Pauls. People say when you find two people who are alike, they argue and quibble. They don't learn to let go, they micro manage and cause issues and friction, and the frustration boils over.

My MD, Adele, has some similarities to me, but in the main she is quite different. That's a good thing. She brings perspective to things that I would normally have gone charging in at, she asks questions and challenges me on situations where I thought my way was the right way. She has changed and altered my take on things.

You don't want a carbon copy of yourself or a nodding dog; you want and need someone who will disagree with you, challenge you, and improve the decision-making process as a result.

A lot of business owners are not great at critical analysis, ie looking at both sides of the story. You are used to doing things your way and making decisions in your business, so a leader who is not identical to you will improve your skills in your leadership toolkit and make you a better businessperson. A leader with a different point of view will improve a business owner's empathy, self-regulation or self-awareness. In other words, they will improve the business owner's emotional intelligence (EI).

EI is a vastly underrated attribute to have as a leader. It was first brought to mainstream attention in 1995 by Daniel Goleman, but it goes back as far as 1964 in a paper by Michael Beldoch. I'm not going to go into too much detail regarding EI; suffice to say that the best leaders have a good understanding of EI and score highly in the attributes of social skills, empathy, self-regulation, self-awareness and motivation.

What to look for in a potential leader

Live and breathe the organisation

It's hard to get good staff, let alone great staff, so if you can get someone who is perfectly aligned to the company's vision, values and beliefs, then they already show a huge amount of potential to become a leader.

If you have a great training and development process, you can teach competency and make people capable, but one thing you cannot do is force them to believe in what you believe. They must do that on their own. Vision is so important to the success of a company. Having aligning values and getting buy in from the staff makes the leader's job much easier.

Focus on potential, not performance

I say this because not everyone performs at their best from day one. In order for your staff to be the best versions of themselves, they may need years and years, so if you are looking for leaders who are performing at their best, appreciate that it may be a lengthy process. Ultimately you may not identify that person.

Potential is a totally different thing. You want someone who has room to grow and, more importantly, is willing to grow. This is not hard to identify. Look for people who are keen to learn, hungry and determined to make themselves better at their job.

The desire to be better at their job is the underlying tone of a true leader. They accept they are not the finished article, they accept they have a way to go, and they always strive to be a better version of themselves. If you identify someone who shares your vision then you really don't have to worry about them making any decision that would put your company, you or your reputation in jeopardy.

I share the same vision and values as my MD, Adele, so I'm completely at ease with her making decisions in the business. I never second guess her as I know she will always have the company, me and the staff's best interests at heart in the way she makes her decisions. I never have to worry that she will do something that isn't aligned with my beliefs or the company's beliefs: 'Be better'. That allows me to work on new ventures and look for opportunities, which in turn produces more income for the business. It's a win-win.

Emotional intelligence

In a nutshell, EI is the capacity to recognise emotions in yourself and others. It stands to reason that if you can connect with others on an emotional level, you will achieve a better relationship and therefore better results. People who don't connect or realise when their colleagues or employees are struggling will be seen as non-empathetic.

Have you heard comments such as 'He doesn't get me', 'He doesn't know what I'm going through' or 'She doesn't understand'? Sound familiar? It may be that the employee making the comments is just venting and the person they're criticising does understand or get them, but in my experience, if your staff are saying things like this consistently, they're not the issue. It's your business leader's lack of emotional understanding.

Improving your leaders' EI and their understanding of your colleagues will improve your business relationships and make your staff feel connected to them. Look for potential leaders with high levels of EI.

Right, enough of the wishy-washy American stuff, back to reality.

Communication skills

Great leaders are great communicators. If you look at business leaders, and even look outside the world of business and into sport, the best performers/leaders in any team are good communicators. Martin Johnson, the captain of England when the team won the Rugby World Cup in 2003, was a great communicator, and a fantastic leader. He led from the front, but more importantly he got buy in from the other players. Communication played a huge part in this.

If your leaders are quiet and meek, then they can't help your people buy in to your vision and values. People buy from people they trust, and quiet people can take a lot longer to establish that trust.

Communication doesn't have to be one way. Great leaders ask for feedback and listen as much if not more than they talk. I have always felt that a message loses its impact if it goes on longer than it needs to. Great communicators use few words, but when they speak those words, they have the greatest of impact. Remember, you're not expecting to have a Winston Churchill-type orator in your business, someone who stirs the soul, but someone with potential to encourage others to become the best versions of themselves.

Calmness

All great leaders are calm in difficult situations. They always seem to know what to do, have the right answers; they never sweat or get flushed...

Or do they?

Of course they do; they just don't show it. Everyone gets nervous before a big event or decision, it's human nature. Anyone who says otherwise is saying so for bravado. The difference is that great leaders understand that by being calm, they instil confidence in their followers. No one wants to follow a leader who panics and seems flustered and unsure what to do.

I've been in situations in business, sport and life where I didn't have all the answers, didn't know what to do, but one thing I never did was show panic. I calmly addressed the situation, and if I needed a bit more time to review it, I'd take more time. I made sure that I made the right decision and didn't get rushed into things when I didn't have the full facts.

This attribute of calmness while under fire is an important one for a leader, and if any of your staff show it, they are on their way to becoming a great leader. But be mindful that there is a difference between calmness and not caring. I've witnessed some people reacting to a situation with apparent calmness, when in actual fact they just didn't care.

Challenge them

You want the best person and the best fit for your business, don't you? The only way for anyone to constantly improve is to be challenged. In sport, you get better by playing better teams or training with better people. You get better at school as the content to learn gets harder and the exams more challenging. Challenge helps you grow and improve.

If you do the same process or role over and over again, you will become more effective and efficient at it, but you won't feel challenged. In all likelihood, you will become bored or complacent. All the leading motivational theorists state that self-actualisation, achievement, attainment or ambition, ie becoming better and progressing, is what motivates people, and that's how you get the best from them.

Challenge and push your potential leader to be better, but don't overwhelm them and dump a lot of responsibility and pressure on them. Make sure they have had the training and development they need to achieve the organisational goals.

Empowering someone and abdicating your responsibility are two different things. Get the former right and it will enhance the confidence of a valuable staff member to leader status, but the latter will demotivate, demoralise and potentially force the employee to leave the company. This is where your EI needs to be prevalent so you can empathise with others and are aware of your own strengths and weaknesses. Abdication of your responsibilities will be seen as a negative so make sure you are clear when you delegate responsibilities to your potential leader.

Make sure your potential leader is challenged properly. An increase in workload and pressure will show how well they can cope, but ensure the work is more challenging than they have been doing. Just dumping twice as much monotonous work on someone will seem challenging, but it won't get the grey matter moving and motivate them.

When you challenge your potential leader, you need to make their tasks more difficult and put slight pressure on them to see how they react. It may seem cruel, but as the saying goes, you have to be cruel to be kind. It's no good telling your child he or she is excellent at football, and then he or she is made to look a fool on the pitch. Your child will never thank you for that, and the same applies in business. People can lose their jobs if they make mistakes, so it's even more important to have the right person in the leadership role and challenge them to make sure they are performing.

Develop a training programme

Any training and development programme needs to be thoroughly planned and documented, no matter who is being trained. I myself have an ILP and I follow it religiously. I also make sure I'm accountable to Adele, my MD, and my better half at home, Gemma. They make sure I complete the courses I start, upskill myself in the ways that I have identified and progress towards a goal. At the moment, I am working towards a master's in leadership. It's something I'm passionate about, so I want to know more.

Ensure your leader has an ILP, and no matter how small the milestones may be, document them in the greatest of detail. I'm a huge fan of an ILP as it shows where I am on my progression journey. Do I need any additional support and can I celebrate any mini successes?

Your training programme for your leader needs to challenge them and push them to achieve their own and the company's goals. Never devalue your company goals to make them easy for the leader to attain. The leader needs to up his or her game to meet the organisational goals and standards rather than the other way around.

When you're developing a training plan, communication is the key. You need to have open channels with the prospective leader. I personally would sit down with them and go over all the training, what I expect them to achieve, and how and why that fits into the business strategy. I believe you get better buy in from all staff once they can see where they fit into the overall picture. This isn't a Mr Miyagi situation where you don't tell the person why they are doing something, but still hope it all comes off and fits together after several months of training and development. Communicate with your potential leader, be open and honest, and support them as they grow and progress.

What happens if you train them and they leave?

Good question, but what happens if you don't train them and they stay? You only want the best people working for you, otherwise you will be running a work crèche, babysitting everyone, wiping arses, sticking up for slackers. If you want demotivated staff, poor customer service, constant firefighting, no time to yourself and probably no profits, then don't train and develop your staff into becoming leaders. But I very much doubt that will appeal to any of you.

Creating a leader in your business will not happen overnight. It will be a long, hard process, and there is a real risk that they will leave as soon as you have trained them up, but training and development is the only way you can create the culture of becoming better. You will be creating a conveyer belt of leaders in the business, and even if some do leave, it's still far better than having a team of demotivated, uninspired plodders.

Leadership is turning vision into reality using influence to create followers.

Learn to let go

Probably the hardest thing I ever had to do in business was let go and trust my staff. It goes against most primal needs as I always want to feel in control, successful and in charge. I was arrogant in that I thought no one could do the job better than me, and in some respects I was right, but in others I was clearly wrong. If you ask my staff, I'm sure they will say I was very wrong.

I felt that my staff wouldn't care and have the same passion that I had. Again, in some instances, that was true. The question I had to ask myself was 'Will the increased level of passion I have guarantee me more business?' Of course not, so why would I continue to struggle to do everything? It wouldn't get me more business; all it would do is stress me out. I didn't have a business, I had a job.

If I had recruited correctly in the first place, which certainly didn't happen, then the staff would have had the same vision, values and beliefs as myself and would ultimately have done the job as well, if not better. I have now created a culture in Castledene that I am proud of in that all the staff do share my business vision, values and beliefs.

Letting go is definitely more of a mind-set than a physical issue, although the sweaty palms and sleepless nights I had when I first did it might have told a different story. Understand that your new leader will make mistakes. They will mess up and you will feel like you want to take back control from them. Don't. If you pick nothing else up from this chapter, please learn to trust your leader's ability in doing their job. If you have recruited well, trained and developed them, and they share the company's values, beliefs and vision, they will in time grow into the leader you want.

No one plays football on a Sunday morning and signs for Sunderland the next week. In fact, no one wants to play for Sunderland, but that's a different matter. Everyone needs time to learn, grow and make mistakes. Of course, you don't want your leader to make too many mistakes, so prepare them as well as you can to take over your organisation, but if you delegate and give them more responsibility, they will screw up from time to time. You just have to accept that.

The pros of having a leader in the business far outweigh the cons of going through the growing pains – not that Castledene had many growing pains in Adele's leadership journey. It's actually quite satisfying seeing your employee getting better and better each day and becoming the leader that you had hoped for. Did Adele make mistakes? Of course she did. Did she learn from them? Yes, definitely. At times I wanted to take back some aspects of the role and thought I could do a better job, but that would have demotivated Adele and sent out the wrong message. Instead, I sat back and let her grow into the role to such an extent that she is now a better manager than I could ever hope to be. I have been there to support her in any way I could, but I let go, let her get on with it, and was patient.

Let everyone know you have a leader

This shows to your leader that you trust them and empower them to run your organisation. You may think behind closed doors that your leader is running the business, but nothing will say it more positively than when you as the business owner give all the credit to them, both publicly and privately. You will get massive buy in and appreciation from your leader, and if you systemise the business effectively and train and develop them, then you can be confident that they will be in a position to run the business.

For example, when anyone wants to talk about a new opportunity or sell me something, I point them in the direction of Adele and she will filter the opportunities and present any to me that may need my approval to take to the next level. I actually have the attention span of a goldfish, especially regarding things such as new IT or phones, so I'm not the best person to be looking at them. While they are imperative to an organisation, I literally have zero interest in them. As Adele is more hands on and operational as a leader, she filters the various options, comes up with a top three list, and then we speak about it. This lets everyone know that Adele's the right person – the leader – to deal with. And once something new is implemented and working well, I let everyone know that Adele deserves all the praise.

Five levels of leadership

While theories are great, unless they have been put into practice, they are just that: theories, unproven and untested. There are a lot of theories in leadership and management, but the best one I've read and implemented is the five levels of leadership by John Maxwell. It's basic in its structure, but it's accurate and opens our eyes as to where we are as a leader.

John Maxwell is a leadership and management expert. In essence, his five levels of leadership relate to the stage you are in your leadership and management career. Many never get past level 2, and that's fine, but you will be looking for at least level 4 in your potential business leaders.

Level 1 – position

This is the lowest level of leadership – the entry level. People who make it only to level 1 may be bosses, but they are never leaders. They have people that work underneath them, not team members. They rely on procedures, processes, policies to control the staff. The staff will only follow them because they have to.

Position is the only level that does not require ability and effort to achieve. Anyone can be appointed to a position. This means that position is a fine starting point, but every leader should aspire to grow beyond level 1.

Level 2 – permission

Making the change from position to permission is a person's first real step into leadership. Leadership is all about influence, and when a leader learns to perform on the permission level, everything changes. People will now start to follow the leader because they want to, not because they have to.

When people feel liked, cared for, included, valued and trusted, they work together with their leader and each other. And that can change the entire working environment. People go along with leaders they get along with.

Level 3 – production

Good leaders always make things happen. They get results. They can make a significant impact on the business. Not only are they productive individually, but they are also able to help the team produce. No one can fake level 3. Either you're producing for the business and making money or you are not.

Level 4 – people development

At level 3, the emphasis is on personal and business results. The ability to create a highly productive team, department, or business indicates a higher level of leadership ability than most people display, but to reach the upper levels of leadership and create elite companies, leaders must transition from producers to developers.

Why? Because people are any organisation's most appreciable asset.

Level 5 – the pinnacle

Very few people ever reach level 5, it's a very rare occurrence. This level is a cumulation of the preceding four levels. But it also requires an increased level of natural ability and talent.

Leaders that reach level 5 create a legacy of leadership in the business that they work in. These types of leaders stand out from everyone else, they are head and shoulders above everyone else and create an environment that works to everyone's advantage.

It's a pleasure to work with and for these leaders. Level 5 leaders have an influence that transcends the business and can work in pretty much any industry and any business.

TASK LIST – LEADERSHIP

- Identify the need for a leader in your business, and it isn't you
- Do you have that potential leader in your business?
- If you don't, map out when and how you can recruit them: finances, timings, etc
- Identify your own weaknesses and work on developing them into strengths – if you are weak at financial management, for example, then look to improve

- Lead by example with a cool head and communicate
- Use the five levels of leadership as a guide and try to work your way through the levels

NINE

PROSPECTING

Prospecting is the lifeblood of any business. If you don't prospect, then you won't grow. Sure, landlords or vendors may come to you, but they won't be beating down the door to experience the award-winning quality of your business if you don't contact them.

Landlords are what I affectionately call 'sticky' in that it takes a lot for them to leave an agent. In the main, they like things safe and don't like to take risks, although it could be argued that by getting into the property industry, they have already taken a risk. Another problem is that some vendors are easily swayed by the lower-end agents over-valuing properties and saying anything to get their business. You need to prospect to tease the landlords and vendors away from their current agents.

There is an argument that says you shouldn't prospect; it's not ethical or morally right to 'steal' landlords or vendors away from their current agent. It's not a good argument, and it's one that I completely disagree with.

I have two counter-arguments:

- If an agent is doing everything right, then they will have nothing to worry about. No one will be able to tempt a client away from an agent who is giving amazing value.

- Everyone thinks it's fine to advertise. At Castledene, we advertise on a daily basis. We tell people what we do, we have stickered-up cars, we have signs on our offices, we have logos on our business cards, we have company Facebook pages – the list goes on and on. If we didn't want to attract business, then we wouldn't do the above. So if this is fine, why is sending a prospect a letter or phoning them out of order?

What is prospecting?

There are many definitions, but the one I like is:

Identifying potential customers by any means of communication.

You are looking for customers, new and old, and trying to connect with them. It may be someone you did business with in the past, maybe someone who has never heard of you, it makes no difference – it's about getting business.

It always surprises me that most – and I mean more than 90% of agents – don't prospect. By the way, I don't classify putting a leaflet up in your window saying 'Landlords wanted' or 'Let us sell your property' as prospecting. How many times has a landlord or vendor walked into your agency and said, 'Hi, I wasn't really looking for an agent, but I saw your poster and thought I'd come in and give you all my business'? It just never happens.

Why don't agents prospect?

They're not sure what to say or do. I get it, I really do. Some people have never been thrown in at the deep end and had to prospect before, so they literally don't know what to say. Couple that with the fact that most letting agents are not very salesy, it's no surprise they get tongue tied or feel anxious when speaking to people.

This is most certainly a mental block. The words are the easy bit. There are only a certain number of situations you can come across, so prepare some phrases to counter them. At Castledene, we only have about a dozen phrases that our staff memorise or have in front of them, so whatever the prospect says, they will be able to counter it or answer their query effectively and professionally.

When I speak to a great salesperson, I'm in awe of them. I love listening to them. Sometimes what they are selling is secondary to their pitch. Just to see and hear them in full flow is great.

Do you think they were that good the first time they ever pitched? Of course not. They had to work at their craft, the same as anything in life. They had to perfect it with scripts, role plays, etc, and you have to do the same. Role play with your managers, your staff, whomever you can. 'Get comfortable with feeling uncomfortable' is the best way to put it. That way you will get used to the pain.

A good analogy is taking a hot bath. It's really uncomfortable when you first get in, but after a short period of time, you get used to it.

It's the same with prospecting and trying out new phrases and sales pitches.

They haven't got the time. This is one of the worst excuses I've ever heard. Of course they've got time – it's basically code for 'I'm not organised' or 'I don't prioritise prospecting highly enough'.

Let's be honest about it – and don't kid yourself – if you don't like prospecting, 'I haven't got time' is a handy excuse. It's all about priorities and what you think is important, and one of the criteria for determining if something is important is how much you enjoy it. We all know prospecting is important, but many people confuse importance with feeling comfortable doing something.

As business owners, especially in a volatile industry such as property, we need to focus on attracting new business. That doesn't mean we forget about servicing our current clients – we can do both at the same time, but we always need to dedicate part of every day to gaining new customers.

Fear of rejection. This is a real reason why people don't prospect. No one likes being told to 'Sod off' or 'Never phone again'. It's human nature and I don't blame them.

The thing to do is to weigh the one-off 'Never phone me again' against the risk of not having enough business to continue operating. That might seem a little over the top, but it's not. If you don't prospect and your competitors do, then it won't be long before this has a huge financial impact on you and your business.

Life is all about choices, and the choices we make are all about priorities. We make choices every single day based on what's important to us. Do we have one more bar of chocolate or do we want to be thin? Do we have one more glass of wine or do we want a clear head in the morning? Do we want to say what we think to our boss and end up in an uncomfortable conversation with them? We will always place some things above others.

Prospecting *must* be placed at the top of your priorities. It's the be all and end all of the business, so bear in mind that rejection isn't the worst thing to fear. Getting a no is an everyday occurrence, or it will be in a progressive and forward-thinking business. Pushing the envelope and trying to grow is not easy, but some rejection beats the alternative – no business at all.

Tips to get over rejection

Are you a mind reader? Can you see into the future? Can you say with 100% certainty that you know what people are thinking all the time? Of course not, so how do you know that a prospect doesn't need your service or want your help? Give them a ring – you may surprise yourself. Have the attitude of wanting to help people, and by calling them, you can do just that. Give them a top-class service and help solve their issues.

Shift the focus to the activity, not the result. Yes, getting business is always important, but if a successful call gets business, then surely the opposite is true when you don't get business. By definition, that's a failure. But that's not true and it shouldn't be looked at like that. You could be warming a lead up for many months to come.

At Castledene, we have sometimes spoken to landlords and vendors for years before they gave us their business, but we didn't class it as a failure when we didn't get their property after the initial phone call. From a psychological perspective, if you change the focus from the result to the activity, you won't be as disappointed when you don't take forty properties on with forty calls. If you call prospects to a consistently high standard, then the results will come in.

Analyse the calls. How can you ensure the quality of your calls is high?

There are three parts to a call:

- **The beginning** – how to open up the conversation. What ice breakers are you using?
- **The content** – how do you build rapport and get that connection?
- **The lasting impression** – what can you say or do at the end of the call to make the prospect a fan?

All conversations will be different as people are all different, and the prospects will have different wants and needs. In the main, if you follow the same basic rules, you can't go far wrong. It's all about tweaking and improving phrases and sentences to make the next conversation the best one yet.

Practise on prospects who don't matter

In fact, all prospects matter, but some matter more than others. Some make you more nervous and put you off your game, for example the ones with large portfolios or expensive properties, etc. Others are easy to talk to and want you to succeed.

I remember when I first set up in business and I was phoning around as many landlords as possible to try and get their business, I met a nice old fellow who had a couple of properties. I was so nervous, I fluffed all my ill-prepared lines, and I think I even gave him some wrong information at one point.

About half way through the meeting, he said, 'You seem nervous, son.' I told him I had just set up and really wanted this to work. He then said, 'Well, if you are prepared to put yourself through this, then you really must want it. That shows me you will look after my properties – you can have them.'

I was blown away, but he had really warmed to me. My nervousness had shown a sort of vulnerability, I guess. This doesn't work for all prospects – some will see nervousness as a sign of weakness and some won't, but you won't be able to practise and practise in a dark room until you are ready to be rolled out and unleashed on the prospects. You need to cut your teeth and practise in the real world.

The best prospects to practise on are the ones you already have a relationship with and know pretty well. They won't judge you – much – and they aren't likely to be rude or give you a hard time.

Who are these prospects? Current landlords or vendors you have done a great job for. People who are happy with your service. Don't jump into 'Can I have your property?'; make sure you talk to them the same way you would a cold lead. This is practice and you need all you can get.

Objections

The scariest aspect of any call is the objection. Pretty much all of us want to be liked, and fear of objection is the reason we don't call. But we can become better equipped to overcome any objections we encounter in prospecting calls.

Clarify. Understand what the issue is. You can't overcome anything unless you understand it. Make every effort to see it from the prospect's point of view and use empathy.

Discuss. Have a chat about the issue. Get all the points. In my experience, the customer is almost never right. If I had to put a figure on it, I would say around two out of ten may be correct. That's not me saying my company is great, or my customers are poor; it's about my employees understanding the process more.

Diffuse. This is where EI plays a huge part. Don't get upset if they have a valid point or they say something that is hurtful about your company. Try to defuse the situation.

Move forward. You can only move forward if you have understood the prospect's issues and overcome them. You can't say 'Whatever... now can I have your business?' It just won't have the desired effect, unless your desired effect is to leave a poor impression.

Purposeful practice

When you are given an objection, it will in 99% of cases be predictable. It will be because the prospect:

- Had a bad experience with you
- Thinks your services are too expensive
- Is 'just looking'
- Can get a better deal elsewhere
- Needs to do work on the property
- Is loyal to a certain agent

With the above in mind, or any objections you have come across more than once, write down your responses to each one and practise them until they roll off the tongue and become second nature.

Have you ever wondered why some people seem to come across so well in a difficult situation over and over again? In rugby or football, some people seem to have so much time on the ball, despite actually having the same time as everyone else. This is because of a process called myelinisation, and while I won't go into detail in this book, it's a fascinating subject and proves that purposeful practice is the key to improving our hard and soft skills.

The more you practise overcoming objections, the better you will be at it. I've been in prospecting sessions with my staff where I've cringed at some of the things they have said, but roll forward a few months and I've been genuinely blown away by how well they come across. Every time I improve the prospecting sessions by adding new phrases or techniques, I can see them looking uncomfortable, but give it a few days and the new technique becomes second nature.

Consistency

Not only does consistency make you better at something, but it also has a profound effect on the results. The more you do something, the better you get at it, and the more time people have to get to know you and trust you. People only do business with people they trust, and one phone call every twelve months is not enough to build rapport and trust with someone.

Regular contact with prospects is literally non-negotiable in our industry. Make sure your staff speak to prospects as often as they can to build relationships. Even if prospects aren't ready to come across, don't give up on them. It doesn't mean they don't want to use your agency; it means they aren't ready right now.

CASE STUDY - A COSTLY MISTAKE

At Castledene, we had a landlord who had five properties in total. We managed two of them and he managed the other three. We did a good job for him, got him great tenants, and he never heard from us. Why would he?

Then we started to prospect him, and he said, 'I've just given my other three properties to another agent.' We asked why, and he said he never heard from us, while he'd had a letter every few weeks from this other agent. Despite us doing a great job for him, he'd given his business to someone else. That hurt and was difficult to take, but it was our own fault. We should have kept in touch more, even if it was a call once a month to see how things were. We even knew he had other properties but we didn't ask to take them on, so we deserved to lose them.

Prospecting strategies

There are lots of strategies to choose when it comes to prospecting, so where the hell do you start? Do you go down the Facebook route and try to become Mark Zuckerberg? Do you make videos *a la* Steven Spielberg? Should you become the Wolf of Wall Street and sell, sell, sell? Can you become a social butterfly and network like crazy? The answer is all and none of them.

Let me explain. You don't need to be Zuckerberg or Spielberg to come up with a great strategy. It doesn't have to be complicated, you just need to pick the one(s) that will give you the best results and do it consistently, and it will deliver you the right results.

We only have three main strategies at Castledene. That's all we need. I've tested and tweaked things over the years to find the strategies that give us the best return on investment, and it is without doubt the following three.

Phone calls

A good old-fashioned phone call cannot be beaten. Nothing gets you more results quicker than this. That's a fact. Not Facebook, not content marketing, not letters, not leaflets – nothing.

Making a connection with people is one of the main reasons I got into business, and that connection must be one of trust. People only do business with people they trust. They don't even have to like them, but they have to trust them. Of course, liking *and* trust is the ultimate aim.

Facebook

This has to be one of your strategies. The amount of information you can deliver quickly on Facebook is exceptional. Pretty much everyone I know has a Facebook account (and uses Facebook on a daily basis).

There are two really good ways to get information to a vendor or landlord on Facebook.

Targeted ads. This is where you design an appealing advert to drive people to your website, on which you need to have an online valuation tool to give them an immediate valuation. In return, they will leave their email address and phone number.

The great thing about this is that you get valuation leads at all times of the day, morning, noon and night. They just land in the email inbox and your staff can follow them up. But don't think everyone who requests an online valuation is currently looking to move. I estimate only around 10% are, but that doesn't stop you having an email nurture sequence with them over a period of time, offering them value and content so when they are ready to move, they come to you.

One issue with the online valuation tool is that often you get false email addresses or mobile phone numbers entered as the prospect knows it's a marketing funnel.

Carousel advert. This is a great way to get more accurate data from the prospect. You have five or six good-quality properties on a carousel-type advert, suggesting that if the prospect wants more information, they complete the Facebook form. Facebook automatically pulls up the email address and mobile telephone number from the information the prospect used when they signed up for an account.

A prospect can still alter the information at the form stage, but it happens much less frequently than it does with targeted ads. Again, the leads just land in your inbox, but in my experience, you need to be contacting the person within an hour of them completing the form. Quite often, they forget they requested more information if you leave it longer.

Letters and leaflets

One of the most controversial prospecting strategies is letters and leaflets, splitting opinion 50/50. To the 50% of people who say letters don't work, I'd reply that the message they are sending is wrong. It's that simple.

If you are saying the same as all your competitors, for example 'Dear Sir, I noticed your property is empty. I'm great, so let me manage it for you', it's not going to work. You need to be original and offer value.

In Castledene letters, we have a four-step ladder that goes along the lines of:

- Letter 1 – hey, how are you doing? Best of luck with your property, we're here to help and add value if you need us.
- Letter 2 – your property's still not let? That's surprising. Have you thought about doing this or that?
- Letter 3 – I'll bet you are really frustrated now. We would love to help. Give us a call.
- Letter 4 – what you are doing clearly isn't working. You need a change in agent, and we can help.

Obviously, there are a lot more influencing techniques that go into it, but you get the basics. We don't go in for the same old hard sell on day one. That stuff never works. You can't go up to a man or woman in a pub, tell them you love them, want to get married and have three babies, and expect it to work. You need to gain and build trust. They must like you first. You need to offer added value.

It's the same with leafleting. If you just show photos or awards you have won, don't be surprised when people don't call. Put yourself in the prospect's shoes. What do they want as a seller of a property or a landlord? They want their home rented or sold for as high a price as possible as quickly as possible. That's all they care about, so show them you can do it. On your leaflet, show five or six properties you have sold or rented and say how quickly you managed it. People will associate you with speed, and the main two drivers of any house sale are speed and highest price.

These strategies work for Castledene, but the ones that work for you may be different for various reasons:

- Location – people in some areas react better to certain strategies.
- Finances – you might not have the finances to pursue a certain type of strategy. Start small and work your way up.
- Staffing – to be blunt, your staff (or you) might not be good enough. You can either get good enough or try another strategy.
- Understanding – some of the strategies can be complicated, especially the techier ones such as Facebook.

Where do you get prospects' info from?

If you are established, the amount of information you can dig up from your CRM system will be huge. Every single past valuation, withdrawn property, customer – follow up literally every single transaction you have made with someone. Some people say you should go back two years, but I've heard that the sweet spot is three to four years when prospects are coming to the end of a mortgage period. There is no hard and fast rule. At Castledene, we start with the most recent and work backwards, phoning everyone we have a number for.

If you are not established, in order to get phone numbers, you will have to think outside the box. Yes, send letters and leaflets, etc, but they're not great for getting the vendor's or landlord's phone number. Every single tenant who comes to you, ask them for at least three, possibly five years' housing history. Insist on the landlord's phone number. You can then phone the landlord(s) up and offer your services.

Content marketing

This strategy without doubt gets results, but it does take a while and you won't get instant wins. Or if you do, then it's down to luck – which is all a lot of business is.

Content marketing is about giving tons of great content out to the public and becoming the trusted expert in the space that you are in. You gain people's trust by being seen or read as often as possible, the one proviso being that the content must be relevant and accurate. No one wants to read content that's inaccurate or irrelevant to them. The fact that the British public have a love affair with property really works in your favour.

A good friend of mine, Chris Watkins, coined the phrase 'Become the digital mayor of your local town'. With video anticipated to be the medium of choice on social media by 2022, it's a must that you start to use video in your prospecting. This doesn't mean you have to be the world's best interviewer or a natural on the camera; you just need to be authentic. People will connect with authentic people as they will see themselves in that person. We always root for the underdog, so the vast majority of people will be rooting for you.

You will have haters, you will have people trying to pull you down. I had someone troll me on Christmas Day on my profile page – I called him the Grinch and wished him Merry Christmas. Just forget about them and move on. Don't let them spoil a potentially great prospecting strategy.

Tips to becoming a top prospector

Remove all distractions

Sounds obvious, but people will look for any excuse not to actually sit down and do the work.

Statistics suggest that people are up to five times more likely to answer a mobile number than a landline number. We at Castledene give all our managers a prospecting phone and state that they are not allowed to have their emails connected or any apps on the phone. No pinging message alerts or Facebook notifications to distract them.

Explain to the staff that they are not to disturb the prospector under any circumstances. No matter what, they can wait for an hour. Get everyone involved and supporting you in your prospecting efforts. Work with the prospector, not against them.

Make it a daily habit

I know some people like to prospect all day on a certain day, but I don't recommend this for a number of reasons:

- Habits need daily occurrence to become engrained.
- Don't wait a week to phone a prospect – phone them every day if need be.
- Employees won't come to dread the day you prospect. If it's done daily, they will come to accept a small amount of time prospecting.

Start simply

Start off with twenty minutes per day, then increase it to thirty, then forty and so on. It's a bit like going to the gym and trying to bench press your body weight on day one. It isn't going to happen, you need to work up to it. Grow slowly.

Get an accountability buddy

Having someone to hold you accountable always works better than being left to your own devices. You need someone to actually kick your bum if you don't do it. I tell my clients that if they want a friend, they need to phone the Samaritans. I'm here to make them and their business better, not chat about what a lovely weekend they had. You need someone like that holding you accountable.

Reward and replace

Celebrate the little wins. If you hit your monthly target, etc, make a big thing about it, take the staff out for a nice meal. After all, you will have the income to do it thanks to their hard work.

If you or your managers are giving an hour a day to prospecting, you will have displaced an hour's worth of work. It doesn't disappear; it still needs doing, so see if you can delegate it, outsource it or automate it. If you don't, it will eat you up and take your mind away from prospecting. Don't be left feeling guilty about it.

Be imperfect

Understand that you won't be great at prospecting the first time you pick up the phone. You will make mistakes and feel embarrassed from time to time.

If you read my first book, *From Stress To Success*, you will know that I used to be a professional MMA fighter. I would get all worked up about losing, what I would feel and what people would think of me – until the first time I was beaten. Then I felt as if a weight had been lifted from my shoulders and I could now enjoy the sport.

No one is unbeatable at anything, so don't think you have to win every phone call. Take the pressure off yourself, enjoy the process and look at the bigger picture.

Know the benefits

When you appreciate what prospecting will do for your company and how much it will affect the company's income, securing your livelihood, your family's future and keeping a roof over your head, then not doing it will become the most scary thought. It may sound dramatic, but it's realistic. Put an emotional anchor on the success or failure of your prospecting and watch the productivity and intensity increase drastically. Once you care about something, you are much more emotionally connected to it and will give it everything you have.

There you have it: the best prospecting strategy I have come across. I have tested and tweaked everything in this chapter to get it working as efficiently and effectively as possible, and my team and I are constantly improving it. Don't go for big changes, just go for the marginal gains, the incremental alterations that give you 1 or 2% improvements rather than 10%.

Always record the results. At Castledene, we have had some surprising results from strategies and actions that we would never have recognised had we not had the data to evidence it. These results changed our outlook on certain aspects of prospecting, like:

- **Changing to mobile phone** – this increased the prospect answer rate by just over 300% consistently over a period of time
- **Letter ladder** – we changed the way we wrote letters and improved the response rate by nearly 500%
- **Leafleting** – we changed the leaflet format to show how quickly we sold properties and the response rate increased by 200%
- **Messaging** – when we left a message, we changed the wording and got pretty much an instant 300% increase in returned calls

Even though I consider my team pretty damn good at prospecting, we are always testing and trying to improve what we are currently doing.

The secret to prospecting is consistency. To get the best from your chosen prospecting strategy, you need to be doing it every single day, not twenty minutes here and there. You won't get a six pack by eating great food every other day, cakes and biscuits on your off days. Prospecting needs to be engrained into your business and as much a part of your agency as opening the doors in the morning. Do that and you will have more business than you can handle.

TASK LIST - PROSPECTING

- Pick your strategies under the 50/30/20 way of thinking (ie 50% of your time and energy spent on one strategy, then 30% on the next, then 20% on a third)
- Understand them
- Roll them out
- Be consistent
- Measure the results so you know what works and what doesn't work
- Collect every piece of data possible

CONCLUSION

That's the Agency Roadmap: the step-by-step journey to building a profitable and sustainable agency. It breaks down the smoke and mirrors of how business should work and gives you definitive actions and lists of what you need to do to make sure your company is the best it can be. Reread the chapters if necessary and don't miss anything out. It all works together like a spider's web to make sure there are no gaps in how you operate.

Imagine reading and implementing all but one of the modules. What's the worst that could happen? Let's take financial management as an example. Everything is great, your staff are performing well, you are prospecting daily, but you lack financial clarity in your business. You think you are making money, so you make an expensive decision affecting your business. All of a sudden, the cash flow dries up, you don't have enough money to pay suppliers, you get calls from the bank to say you have gone overdrawn...

OK, better not leave out financial management. What about training and development? Your staff are pretty intelligent, they should be able to work out how to read a procedure.

Now imagine if something goes wrong and a client leaves. You bring the offending employee into your office for a good old-fashioned dressing down, which would go something like this:

You: 'Why didn't you follow the procedure?'

Employee: 'What procedure?'

You: 'The one in the operations manual.'

Employee: 'Didn't know I had to.'

You: 'You know you should follow it, as per your training.'

Employee: 'What training?'

You: 'Oh yeah!'

Last example, I promise, but this one is probably the most frequently left out. I can't stress how important values and beliefs are. This module is by far the most important of the Agency Roadmap.

Your values and beliefs are everything that you and your company hold dear. They are the moral compass that guides every decision you make. Imagine chasing the money at the expense of your staff or your customers. Imagine recruiting someone who just spoke about how rich they wanted to be and never mentioned customer service or adding value. Imagine writing things like 'If they don't pay the rent, send the lads round' in your procedures. No values? You have no moral compass to guide you. You need them, and your staff need to sign up and operate by them in everything they do, no exceptions.

The modules of the Agency Roadmap can't be taken in isolation or your business won't operate to its full capability. You might operate at 50% or 75%, maybe even 90%, which is pretty good, but are you in business to be pretty good or great? Do you want to build an OK agency or the best in the area? You can only be the best by addressing all the issues in your business, which is why the Agency Roadmap is the ultimate way to take your business from where it is now to where you want it to be.

Do you want to learn more?

If you want to follow my Agency Roadmap in more detail, have access to all the content, tools and tricks contained in the book, and much more, then check out my membership site www.agencyallstaracademy.co.uk

ACKNOWLEDGEMENTS

As with everything that's a lot of hard work such as writing a book, it's never a solo project. It's a team effort.

Although I was the one who wrote the book, the support I have had to be allowed to do this has been huge and a few people deserve a mention:

Gemma – Thanks for being you and running the house with military precision and allowing me to do what I enjoy. Love you, Mrs Paul.

Stephanie, Jack and Bella – You are the reason I do what I do. Daddy loves you all very much and you make me so very proud each and every day.

Adele – Thanks for running and leading the business, which allows me to do things like this. You are one in a million and I can't say thank you enough.

THE AUTHOR

John Paul is an entrepreneur, leader and owner of the Castledene Group, an award-winning sales and letting agency based in North-East England. Widely regarded as one of the leading experts in the property industry, John won the *Sunday Times* Outstanding Contribution to Lettings Award in 2015 and speaks at networking events all over the UK. John has grown Castledene Sales and Lettings into seven branches employing over fifty staff.

John's main passion is business and giving business owners the tools to 'Build a business to create a life'.

John is also on the Board of the Association of Residential Letting Agents (ARLA), representing the North of England.

Success is predictable and it also leaves clues. Having structure and routine in your business gives you the best chance of achieving success. *The Agency Roadmap* does that.

John has three amazing children – Stephanie, Jack and Bella – and a long-suffering but supportive partner, Gemma. They live in Redmarshall in Stockton on Tees.

If you would like to contact John, you can on johnpaul@thecastledenegroup.com

Or if you would like to know more about the Agency Roadmap and how it can help transform your business, then visit www.agencyallstaracademy.co.uk

CPSIA information can be obtained
at www.ICGtesting.com
Printed in the USA
LVHW040021170120
643872LV00016B/1543